THE WORLD OF SCIENCE
PLANTS

THE WORLD OF SCIENCE
PLANTS

DAVID BLACK &
ANTHONY HUXLEY

Facts On File Publications
New York, New York ● Bicester, England

PLANTS

Copyright © Orbis Publishing Limited 1985
Copyright © Macdonald & Co (Publishers) Ltd 1988

First published in the United States of America in
1985 by Facts on File, Inc., 460 Park Avenue South,
New York, N.Y. 10016

First published in Great Britain in 1985 by Orbis
Publishing Limited, London

**Library of Congress Cataloging in Publication
Data**

Main entry under title:

World of Science

   Includes index.
   Summary: A twenty-five volume encyclopedia of
scientific subjects, designed for eight- to-twelve-year-
olds. One volume is entirely devoted to projects.
   1. Science—Dictionaries, Juvenile.   1. Science—
Dictionaries
Q121.J86   1984   500   84-1654

ISBN: 0-8160-1065-X

Printed in Italy
10 9 8 7 6 5 4

Consultant editors
Eleanor Felder, Former Managing Editor, *New Book
of Knowledge*
James Neujahr, Dean of the School of Education, City
College of New York
Ethan Signer, Professor of Biology, Massachusetts
Institute of Technology
J. Tuzo Wilson, Director General, Ontario Science
Centre

Previous pages
Close-up photograph of
dandelion seed-heads
and buttercups in a
grassy meadow.

Editor Penny Clarke
Designer Roger Kohn

CONTENTS

I THE PLANT KINGDOM

2 HOW PLANTS GROW

3 PLANTS WE DEPEND UPON

4 UNUSUAL WAYS OF LIFE

5 THE FUTURE

▲ The pale flower-spike of the autumn lady's tresses orchid which, as its name suggests, flowers later than many orchids.

Note There are some unusual words in this book. They are explained in the Glossary on pages 62–63. The first time each word is used in the text it is printed in *italics*.

1 THE PLANT KINGDOM

INTRODUCTION

The history of plants is a long one, much longer than that of animals. Archeologists have found *fossils* of tiny plants in rocks more than 3,000 million years old. These tiny fossilized plants were the first green conquerors of our planet, and are about the earliest-known forms of life. Much later, some 200 million years ago, came the more familiar plants – larger algae, mosses, ferns, coniferous trees and the great range of flowering plants.

Plants similar to the microscopic fossil plants occur today, they are called blue-green algae. They are found in many places, but especially where other plants cannot survive, such as around the edges of hot springs or on freezing cold Arctic wastes.

The green providers

We tend to take plants for granted, as though they have always been and always will be part of our landscape. Plants certainly provide us with a range of *vegetation*, from cactus semi-deserts to cool green forests – but even more important, we depend on plants to live. Think of all the foods you eat – not only the green foods. It may seem a long way from a plant to a hamburger or milk shake, yet it is only a short step. Hamburger buns, and all the bread you eat, come from the ground up seeds of plants such as wheat and corn. Hamburgers are made from the meat of beef cattle which feed on grass. Milk comes from cows, which again feed on grass. Even the frozen fish sticks you buy in the supermarket came originally from plants. Fish such as cod feed on smaller

fish, which in turn eat microscopic plants that live in the surface waters of the sea. These plants are known collectively as phytoplankton. We also eat a great deal of plant matter in the form of fruits and vegetables. Plant fibres are used to make cloth, either directly from the seed heads of the cotton plant or, indirectly, from the wool produced by sheep. Trees provide timber for building and furniture, and paper for newspapers, books, magazines and wrappings. Many medicines and perfumes are extracted from plants.

But what are plants?

Plants are living things that breathe, grow, multiply and eventually die, just like animals. However, they differ in one main respect from animals: they are mainly fixed, rooted to one spot, and so they are able to perform a unique process known as *photosynthesis*. This process involves the green pigment called *chlorophyll* contained inside plant *cells*. The chlorophyll traps the energy from sunlight which, together with water and a gas called carbon dioxide, the plant converts into simple sugars which allow it to grow. A plant's other main requirement, apart from water, is mineral salts. These are absorbed from the soil via the roots, together with water. Photosynthesis is carried out by all plants except a few that feed on dead matter (*saprophytes*) or on living plants and animals (*parasites*). Fungi (page 10) are well-known examples of saprophytes and the mistletoe and dodder are both parasites (page 58).

World vegetation

The world can be divided into different belts of vegetation, from the poles to the equator. Each belt consists of plants that require similar conditions of rainfall and temperature. If you start at the Arctic the first vegetation you find is a short, turfy *tundra* with no trees. Then comes a wide forest belt of coniferous (cone-bearing) trees, followed to the south by a forest of broad-leaved trees, then grassland, scrub, desert and possibly tropical forest near the equator.

Climbing a high mountain provides a rather similar effect, as you pass through the different vegetation zones. Near the summit, or close to the snow-line if it is a really high mountain, you may find only some tiny, short-stemmed flowers, the high alpines, that have adapted to life in extremes of wind, sun and snow. These are the equivalent of the tundra plants of the world vegetation belts.

▼ Poppies, corn marigolds and ox-eye daisies flower among field grasses in a summer meadow.

THE ALGAE

Botanists, the people who study plants, have divided the plant kingdom into a number of groups, in the same way that zoologists have divided the animal kingdom into groups. The plants of each group all have similarities, such as their shape and structure and the way they reproduce themselves. Some of the simplest plants are the algae.

You may think of algae as small, soft plants without a definite shape, which may sometimes be slimy. This is true of many algae, but the group is so varied that it is difficult to describe a typical algal plant. Algae range in size from one-celled plants you can see only under a microscope, to giant seaweeds over 100 m (328 ft) long. One common feature is that they all grow in or near water, or at least in damp conditions. Algae are the most important group of plants that live in seawater.

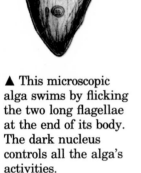

▲ This microscopic alga swims by flicking the two long flagellae at the end of its body. The dark nucleus controls all the alga's activities.

Green algae

There are more *species* of green algae, so-called because of their green coloration, than of any other sort – over 7,000 different species, in fact. One of the most common land-based algae forms green films on the trunks of trees. This alga consists of hundreds of single cells growing close together. (Alga is the singular, algae the plural.)

Some freshwater algae can actually swim. They move through the water by thrashing their flagellae, tiny whip-like 'hairs'. These algae may have only one cell, or many cells joined together which makes them look like minute underwater spacecraft. The green slime that sometimes forms on the sides of fishtanks is an alga made from many cells joined together in long strands.

The green seaweeds are really large forms of algae. A common one is called sea lettuce because its broad, thin, bright green leafy fronds do make it look a little like lettuce. The body of a seaweed is made of different cells: some form the leaf and others form the 'stalk'. At the base of the stem is the 'holdfast', which takes the place of the roots most land plants have.

Green algae reproduce in many ways. Parts of a plant may simply break off to form a new one. Some other plants produce male and female cells which, in the case of seaweeds, meet together in the sea. Sometimes so many of these cells are released that they turn the water green.

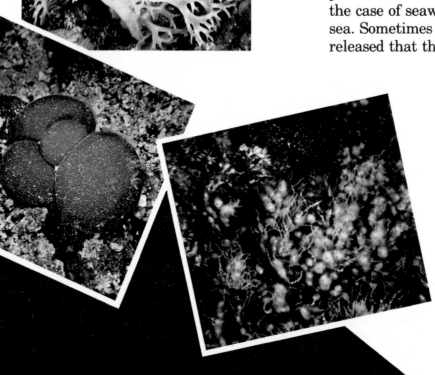

◄ Examples of three types of algae found in the sea. **Top** A red alga that lives in deep water in warm seas. **Middle** Green algae live in shallow seas where the Sun's rays can reach. **Left** A brown alga that lives at medium depths.

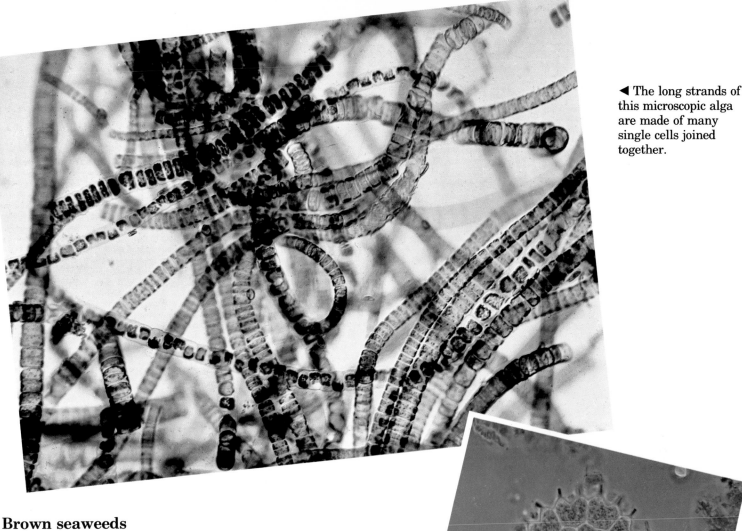

Brown seaweeds

Brown seaweeds are larger than the green ones. They are the slippery ones you find on sea-shores between the high and low water marks. Their brown colour comes from a pigment (called fucoxanthin) which masks the green pigment chlorophyll. Brown algae often have a tough midrib which runs down the centre of the frond. Some types have air bladders to keep them afloat. Brown algae form miniature jungles along the shore which provide shelter for many sea creatures. Along the coast of California are underwater forests made of large brown algae known as giant kelp. The Sargasso Sea in the mid-Atlantic is made up of a huge area of floating brown 'weeds'. Most brown algae are found in cold waters.

Red seaweeds

Red algae contain another kind of pigment (called phycoerythrin) which makes them pink, red or purple. They are generally small plants, often very delicate. Most live in deeper water below the tideline, and are more common in warmer seas.

Useful algae

The tiny green algae that float in the surface waters of the sea are very important in the life of the ocean. They form the first stage in the *food chain* for many marine creatures. Some of the largest whales live on the minute plants and animals that together are called plankton.

Seaweeds are eaten by people, especially in the East in countries such as Japan. Seaweeds are extremely rich in minerals and they taste good. Although people in the West do not eat seaweeds directly, they use them in other ways. A substance called algin is extracted from seaweed and is used to set such foods as ice-cream and sauces. It is also used in the manufacture of many different products – from cosmetics, paints and beer to rubber tyres.

▲ This alga, which is microscopic, is made up of similar cells that have divided and grown into the shape of a ball.

FUNGI

▲ The fairy ring mushroom is common on garden lawns. The hyphae grow outwards from the spore to form a circular mycelium. This dies away at the centre so that the mushrooms grow in a circle. The mycelium of these mushrooms may live as long as 400 years.

The mushrooms you find in the woods in autumn are just one part of one kind of fungus. What you see is the fruiting body or reproductive structure. Most fungi have a fruiting structure of this type, though it varies in size and shape according to the species. Sometimes it has a strong smell that attracts the insects which are necessary to disperse the *spores* that will produce new fungal plants. Many of these fruiting bodies are extremely poisonous to humans.

Plants with a difference

The first thing you notice about a fungus is that it is not green like other plants. This is because it does not have the pigment called chlorophyll used by other plants to make their own food. Instead a fungus gets its nourishment by feeding either on dead plant or animal matter. Most species of fungus feed in this way, although a few feed on living plant or animal tissue. Those feeding on dead matter are called saprophytes, while those feeding off living tissue are called parasites.

The simplest fungi, such as yeast, only have one cell and reproduce by budding off new ones. This process is called asexual reproduction because it does not involve the joining of male and female cells. Yeast is used to ferment wine, make beer and make bread rise. The fluffy mould you find on stale bread or on an old tomato is another kind of fungus.

It is made up of a great many branching threads which tunnel their way through the food supply. Under a microscope you can see that some of the threads have dark rounded tips which contain reproductive spores. When they are ripe, the fungus sheds the spores, which can remain alive for a long time. When a spore lands on a suitable food supply it will grow and develop a new patch of mould.

Fungi such as puffballs and mushrooms produce spores that are the result of the fusion of male and female cells. These spores are shot from the fruiting body in enormous quantities. For example, a common field mushroom can produce 1.5 billion spores in a few days while a bracket fungus can produce 30 billion spores per day!

The secret life of mushrooms

Below ground the fruiting body of one mushroom is connected to the fruiting bodies of other mushrooms by a mass of branching threads known as a *mycelium*. These unseen parts can grow out like a giant underground mould over 15 m (50 ft) wide. The regular growth of a mycelium is best shown by the fairy ring mushroom. At the outer edge of the ring is an area of luxuriant green grass produced by the fungus breaking down food substances in the soil. Just inside this ring, where the mycelium is dense, the mushrooms of the fungus appear, often in a regular ring. Here the grass may be thin, or even prevented from growing by the quantity of mycelium in the ground within the ring.

Certain mushrooms grow close to certain kinds of tree. During the course of *evolution* a close relationship has been built up between these two very different plants. The mycelium of mushrooms actually penetrates the roots of certain trees, including birches, beeches and some conifers. Botanists are not certain just how this relationship works, but it is likely that the fungus provides the tree with essential nutrients that it has broken down from humus in the soil. In turn, through the tree root, the fungus obtains moisture and food substances that it needs.

Fungi good and bad

Fungi cause a great deal of damage and disease by feeding on living plants and animals. Important fungal diseases of plants include the rusts and smuts of cereal crops. Athlete's foot and ringworm are two common fungal diseases of humans.

On the other hand, in many parts of the northern hemisphere, mushrooms and other species of fungi were an extremely important source of food in days when fruit and vegetables were limited to those that could be grown locally. Mushrooms were dried, pickled and cooked in a variety of ways, but it took – and still takes – expert knowledge to tell the edible from the poisonous species.

▲ This mushroom is known as Lawyer's Wig because of the appearance of its peeling cap. It is good to eat and, unlike some other edible mushrooms, is easy to recognize. But, it is not safe to pick any wild mushroom unless you are absolutely sure what they are.

▶ These funnel-shaped *Lentinellus* fungi grow on tree stumps, especially beech.

▼ Earth-balls are related to puffballs, so-called from the clouds of tiny spores that puff out of the ripe mushrooms. The giant puffball can weigh 7 kg (15 lb).

MOSSES

Mosses are another very simple type of land plant. Instead of roots, they have branching threads called rhizoids. Unlike algae, however, they do have a stem with many simple overlapping leaves. Most of the 14,500 species of moss are very small and form tightly packed low-growing clumps. Each clump is made up of many single plants growing closely together. Mosses grow in damp places such as on the banks of streams, or on the undersides of rotting logs. One of the largest mosses is an Australian moss which reaches 70 cm ($27\frac{1}{2}$ in) – a tremendous height for a moss.

A two-part life

Mosses, and related plants called liverworts, have an interesting life history. A typical moss plant is called a *gametophyte* because it forms sex cells or *gametes* at its tip. *Fertilization* takes place in wet weather, because moisture enables the male cells to swim and reach the female ones. The fertilized egg grows into a capsule carried on the end of a stalk which grows up out of the moss plant. This is the second generation of the moss plant and is called a *sporophyte* because it produces spores. In dry weather many tiny spores are released from the capsule. But they need damp ground to develop further. If conditions are right, they grow into a delicate thread-like structure called a protonema. This grows and buds into a typical moss plant and the cycle begins again.

Blanket bogs

Mosses form the main vegetation of boggy regions and are also important in the treeless Arctic tundra. In both habitats mosses of various kinds can blanket hundreds and even thousands of square kilometres. In boggy areas, such as parts of Ireland, the long-dead moss has accumulated to form thick layers of peat which is cut, dried and used as fuel.

▼ The double life-cycle of a moss. The main part of a moss plant is called the gametophyte. It produces male and female sex cells. When these join together at fertilization another kind of moss plant, called the sporophyte, is produced. It often grows out from the gametophyte plant. The sporophyte produces many tiny spores which fall on to the ground and grow up into new gametophyte moss plants.

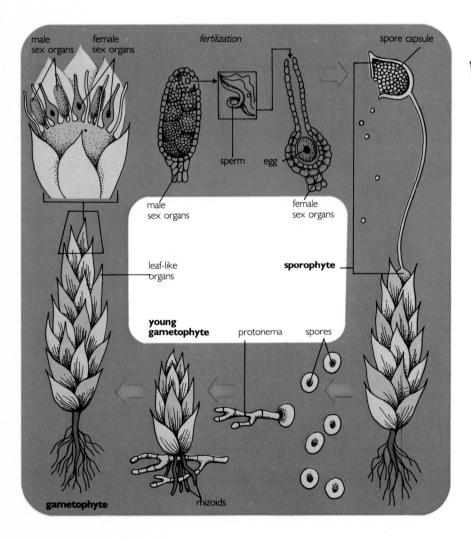

male sex organs   female sex organs   fertilization   spore capsule

sperm   egg

male sex organs   female sex organs

leaf-like organs   **sporophyte**

young gametophyte   protonema   spores

gametophyte   rhizoids

▲ Red-stalked sporophytes growing from the gametophytes of a wood moss.

▲ Sphagnum moss is found on marshy land. It forms peat when it decays.

FERNS

◄ Magnificent giant ferns growing in the warm, moist conditions of a tropical rainforest.

▼ This is the prothallus of a fern much magnified. The tiny hair-like growths anchor it to the ground. The darker patches are the male and female cells. The next stage of the fern's life cycle will grow from a pair of these cells.

Ferns are beautiful plants that generally grow in deep shade. There are about 10,000 different kinds. Most grow in warm wet forests where they can reach a large size. In New Zealand tree ferns can reach heights of 25 m (82 ft).

Life in two parts

Ferns, like mosses, have a two-part life history. The main differences are that the spore-bearing plant is large – it is the plant with leafy fronds that we call a fern – and the plant bearing the sex cells is a completely separate plant. The spores are often contained in spore cases, or *sporangia*, on the underside of the fronds. When the sporangia split open they release many minute spores. The plant that grows from the spores is quite different from a typical fern. It is very small, less than 1 cm (½ in) across, and often heart-shaped. This is the prothallus which bears both male and female sex cells. Again, water is necessary to enable

the male cell to reach the female cell for fertilization.

Some ferns live completely in water. They are free-floating and form thick masses of vegetation with their roots dangling down into the water. Other ferns are *epiphytes* (page 22) and grow on trees and vines, often high up.

▲ The tightly curled fronds of the male fern in spring. They have grown from a prothallus similar to one **above left**.

13

TREES WITH CONES AND NEEDLES

▶ A fine Scots pine growing beside a loch in Scotland. These pines have a reddish bark and pinkish buds from which they get their European name of red pine. The needles are blue-green in colour and grow in pairs. The cones have thick scales and take three years to mature. In the first year they are reddish, in the second green and, finally, in the third year they are brown.

Cone-bearing trees, or conifers as they are generally called, are ancient plants that evolved over 200 million years ago. This was a very long time before the main group of flowering plants appeared on Earth. In Europe the best-known conifer is the Norway spruce. This is the 'Christmas tree' bought by millions of people each year. Conifers are mainly grown for their timber which is called softwood because it is easier to work than the wood of broad-leaved trees which is termed hardwood. Softwood is used for a variety of purposes. For example, some is cut into chips and stuck together with plastic glues to make chipboard, a manufactured wood. Most of the paper we use is made from the wood of coniferous trees.

Cones
The cones are the fruiting bodies of coniferous trees. They develop from tiny flowers. Male and female cones are generally carried on the same tree. The male cones contain pollen sacs. When the

sacs ripen, they release millions of minute pollen grains, the male cells. The pollen is carried by the wind onto the female flowers where fertilization takes place. The small female flowers grow and develop into soft green cones and later into the familiar woody ones, a process that takes about 18 months. The seeds develop on the cone scales and when the weather is dry the cones open and release the ripe seeds. The seeds of conifers have no protective seed pods, so botanists describe the trees as *gymnosperms*. Conifer seeds often have wings which enable the wind to carry them to open ground where they can develop into young seedlings.

Needles
Most conifers are *evergreen*. The needle-shaped leaves or 'needles' do not last forever but live for three or four years before they are shed. However as the needles are shed gradually, and not all at once, the tree remains green. The discarded needles rot very slowly and you will find a thick layer of dry brown needles if you walk through a pine wood.

Many conifers live in dry conditions, either where it is very cold for much of the year, or very hot. The needles, with their thick skins and the breathing pores protected in deep central furrows, enable the trees to save water in the extreme climates in which most conifers grow. The narrow pointed crown and conical shape of many conifers also help prevent the boughs breaking under heavy falls of snow. The larch is one of the few conifers that sheds its leaves each year.

Coniferous forests
Vast coniferous forests are found across the northern hemisphere, in North America and the Soviet Union. They occupy an immense area – 1,500 million hectares (3,700 million acres). The forests are made up mainly of spruces, pines and larches. Many birds and mammals depend on these trees for food and shelter. Birds called crossbills have crossed beaks specially adapted for extracting conifer seeds. In many places conifers are grown in plantations made up of a single kind of tree. Unfortunately,

while these artificial forests provide a good source of timber, they do not provide the varied habitat for wildlife that natural forests provide.

Relatives of conifers
Several other kinds of trees and bushes are related to the true conifers. These include the yew which bears its seeds in pink, fleshy berries. The maidenhair tree, another relative, hardly resembles a conifer at all. It has fan-shaped leaves which it sheds each autumn. It is now very rare in the wild, but it has been planted widely as an ornamental tree, especially in city parks. Although the trees known as cycads look like palms, they bear large cones with seeds sometimes the size of plums.

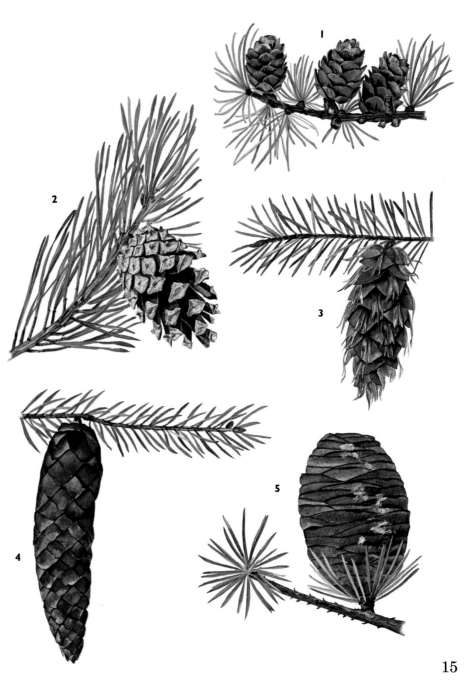

▼ The different species of conifer have very distinctive cones and needles. 1 The European larch has small, fairly soft rounded cones that are pink at first. 2 Scots pines (**opposite**) have large tough cones. 3 The Douglas fir has brown cones with papery scales. 4 The long cylindrical cones of the Norway spruce are a lightish brown. 5 The cedar of Lebanon has round cones with flattened tops and tightly overlapping scales.

▲ Part of the redwood forest in the Sequoia National Park, California. Forests like this once covered most of the northern coastal area of California.

Along the coast of northern California, where the climate is cool and moist, grow huge stands of the largest trees in the world – the sequoias. There are two kinds of sequoia. The largest is the famous redwood tree, which is the tallest tree in the world. The largest specimen is 111.6 m (366 ft) tall, about the size of a 36-floor skyscraper. The other sequoia, although technically called *Sequoiadendron*, is generally just called the big tree because it is the biggest in terms of its overall size. The largest is nearly 83 m (272 ft) high and nearly 10 m (32 ft) thick at the base.

Sequoias have become rare because their timber is strong, attractive and resistant to decay. Many houses in California are built from their wood. Today sequoias are protected in some 30 national parks, strung along the California coast. They provide a peaceful retreat for the city dweller and a glimpse

of the magnificent forest that once covered most of northern coastal California.

Until the 1950s giant sequoias were thought to be the oldest living trees, some being 3,500 years old. But more recent studies show that another North American conifer, the bristlecone pine from eastern California, is very much older. One living specimen is over 4,600 years old; and one specimen that was cut down was 4,900 years old!

▶ 'The Sentinel', a magnificent old sequoia growing in the Sequoia National Park, California. For centuries these trees provided an important source of timber in the area, and as a result large areas of the original forest were cut down. Now, with the increasing awareness of the importance of conservation, the trees are protected in many national parks.

INTRODUCING FLOWERING PLANTS

Flowering plants dominate the plant life of the Earth. There are some 250,000 kinds, ranging from microscopic water plants called duckweeds to giant eucalyptus trees. Elms, maples and oaks are just as much flowering plants as roses, daffodils and tulips. The earliest fossil evidence we have of these plants dates back 130 million years with types very similar to present-day magnolias – garden shrubs or small trees with large white or pink blossoms. The flowering plants increased slowly but surely, until by 110 million years ago they had pushed out the previously dominant conifers and ferns in many areas.

The pattern of world vegetation we know today is very different from what it used to be. The continents were closer than they are now and the climate changed considerably over millions of years. Sometimes it was hot and wet, at other times it was cold and dry, and accordingly at different times various

▲ Lady's slipper orchids grow wild throughout Europe, Asia and the Americas. (This species grows in the rainforests of Asia.) Some of them are very rare and are now protected.

▲ The sweet violet is one of about 400 kinds of violets that grow mainly in shady places.

▲ The flowers of many gentians are an intense blue. These plants grow high up in mountain pastures and among rocks.

groups of plants flourished or died. For example, the climate of southern England some 45 million years ago was hot and steamy. Evidence for this comes from various fossil plants that grew there. They were like those that grow today in steamy tropical swamps.

What is a flowering plant?
Unlike the seeds of gymnosperms (page 15), the seeds of flowering plants, or *angiosperms*, are protected by a seed case or ovary. This forms part of the flower, which is just a shoot of the plant modified for reproduction. A flower may bear both male and female sex organs.

Another feature of angiosperms is the production of fruits which protect the seed and help in its dispersal.

Among flowering plants there are two subdivisions, the *monocotyledons* and the *dicotyledons*. Cotyledon is the name for the leaf contained inside the seed, the first leaf to appear after *germination*. Monocotyledons include plants such as grasses, sedges, orchids, lilies, tulips, daffodils and palms. When these plants germinate there is only one seed leaf. The mature leaves of these plants also usually have straight or parallel veins. In all other flowering plants, the dicotyledons, two leaves of equal size open out above the ground, and the mature leaves have a net-like arrangement of veins.

TROPICAL RAINFORESTS – PLANTS IN PROFUSION

Satellite pictures of the Earth show the tropical forests of the world as a belt of green, extending no more than 10° of latitude either side of the equator. In this region the climate is hot and steamy and plants grow throughout the year.

In South America the world's largest expanse of forest occupies the basin of the river Amazon and its tributaries. There is also forest along coastal Colombia, through Panama and into southern Mexico. In Africa the main core of forest lies in the basin of another river, the Zaire, formerly the Congo. The third great expanse of forest is in south-east Asia – in Malaysia, southern Thailand, Indonesia and Papua New Guinea. In all there are some 1,000 million hectares (2,500 million acres) of this lush forest which contains more kinds of plants than any other region. For example, in Malaysia there are about 8,000 kinds of forest plants, six or seven times the number found in an equivalent area of Europe.

Forest features
To fly over one of these tropical forests is like travelling over a sea of green. Here and there some giant tree up to 45 m (150 ft) high emerges head and shoulders above the green canopy. Scattered over the canopy some trees are in flower, while others are heavy with fruits. The continuous rolling canopy forms a tight green patchwork made up of the crowns of trees, some 30 m (100 ft) high. Beneath

▼ Breadfruit is a native plant of the forests of Malaysia. The starchy fruits are eaten raw or cooked, or ground and used to make bread.

◄ The lush vegetation of this tropical mountain forest contains many palms, indicating how common they are in tropical regions.

▲ A pool in the Amazon basin with marsh vegetation growing in the foreground. In the background the trees of the tropical rainforest come down to the water's edge.

these are smaller trees and palms with narrow crowns some 15 m (50 ft) high, and beneath them, growing close to the forest floor, are shrubs, ferns and many flowering plants. But, because of the dense shade, these understorey plants, as they are called, are generally quite sparse.

▶ A palm tree bud which will soon open into a large flower cluster. There are about 4,000 different kinds of palm tree growing in the tropics.

Special features

Rainforest trees have a shallow root system. Some species have wide, spreading buttress roots to give them support, others have prop roots like the structure of a teepee. The trunks themselves tend to be smooth and straight until near the forest canopy, when they branch out to catch any available light. These trees support many other plants. For example, there are many kinds of woody climbing plants called lianes which twine around or grip the tree trunks and grow upwards towards the light. Some plants called epiphytes actually grow upon the trees. They are not parasites, but use the trees for support. They obtain moisture from rain, by means of special aerial roots, and obtain their nourishment from fallen leaves and other plant debris which gather around their roots. Common epiphytic plants are ferns, mosses, bromeliads and orchids. Bromeliads have close-packed leaves which form a cup to hold water. These miniature pools high up on the trees are the homes of insects and tiny tree frogs.

► Epiphytic ferns growing high up in the forest. They cling to trees only to get light – they are not parasites.

HOW PLANTS GROW

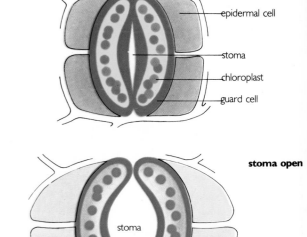

leaf cross section

stomata

stoma closed

epidermal cell

stoma

chloroplast

guard cell

stoma open

stoma

guard cell buckles

LEAVES

Plants breathe through their leaves and also, in a way, feed through them. For the leaves of plants are the food-producing organs, because it is the leaves that contain most of the chlorophyll used in photosynthesis (page 6). In the same way that sugar is a good source of energy for us, the plant sugars produced in photosynthesis give the plant energy to grow. In addition, a plant can make more complicated substances, such as proteins, from its sugars and the mineral salts it obtains from the soil through its roots. Proteins are just one of the many substances needed to make the different cells, the 'building blocks' of which all plants and animals are made.

The structure of leaves

Although leaves have very different shapes, inside they are much the same. The outermost 'skin' of a leaf consists of a single cell layer covered by the cuticle, a thin waxy waterproof layer.

Sandwiched between the upper and lower surfaces of the leaf is a mass of cells called the mesophyll. The upper layers of the mesophyll consist of tall thin cells which contain masses of small, green globular bodies known as *chloroplasts*. This is where photosynthesis takes place. The chloroplasts act like miniature solar panels. They capture and store the sun's energy far more efficiently than anything yet devised by man. Plants look green because the chlorophyll in the chloroplasts absorbs all the colours in the light spectrum well except green. The green is reflected from the plant. Photosynthesis is quite a complicated process and results in oxygen being

▲ Holly leaves have a thick waxy cuticle to prevent water loss. They also have sharp spines to prevent animals from eating them.

▲ Each stoma is bordered by two guard cells which contain chloroplasts. As the guard cells produce sugar by photosynthesis they draw in water from neighbouring cells. This increases the pressure in the guard cells causing them to bulge and the pores to open. Water then evaporates into the air. As the water content of the plant drops, the guard cells shrink and the stoma closes.

released by the plant. Although oxygen is necessary for the plant to breathe, plants also release a good deal to the outside air. Plants, therefore, are also an important source of the oxygen that all living things need to breathe.

Gas exchange

Within the leaves there is a constant exchange of gases from photosynthesis, and from the reverse process known as *respiration*. The amount of air, and therefore the amount of gases required by the plant, is controlled by adjustable pores called *stomata*. They are usually concentrated on the underside of the leaf. Each stoma consists of a pore surrounded by two sausage-shaped guard cells. When the plant has plenty of water the guard cells swell up and the pores open. In dry conditions the guard cells become limp and the pores close to prevent water loss from the plant. The pores are extremely small but there are many of them – up to 250 in one square millimetre of leaf, that is an area about the size of a pinhead.

Other uses of leaves

Just as a healthy plant uses its leaves to make food, it also uses them to get rid of its waste products. *Deciduous* trees, trees

that shed their leaves each year before winter sets in, are a good example of this. The waste substances become concentrated in the leaves and when they drop off the waste products are neatly removed from the plant.

Many climbing plants use modified leaves to grip objects. For example, the tendrils of the common garden pea are really modified leaves which it uses to climb up bamboo canes or wire netting provided by the gardener. Other leaves, such as holly, have spines to stop them being eaten. The stinging hairs of the stinging nettle serve the same function.

The spines of cacti, however, are slightly different. They have replaced leaves, to prevent water loss in the dry climates where they grow, and they also protect the cactus stem which has taken over the work of photosynthesis because there are no leaves to do it.

▲ The attractive 'petals' of dogwood, a North American plant, are actually modified leaves called bracts.

◄ Giant water lily leaves can reach 1.8 m (6 ft) in diameter. They float because their veins form air pockets.

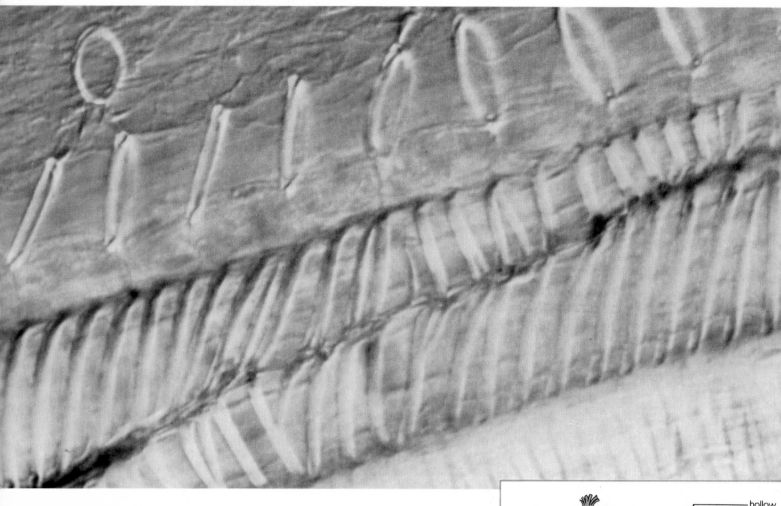

▲ Xylem vessels carry water to all parts of a plant. This photograph, taken through a special very high-power microscope, shows them in longitudinal section.

All plants require water for photosynthesis, but just how does a tall tree, such as a giant redwood, get water from the ground up its trunk to the leaves at the tips of its thinnest branches?

Roots

The process starts with the roots. As well as anchoring the plant in the ground, roots end in fine hairs which take in the water that lies between the soil particles. Even a simple plant such as a grass has a

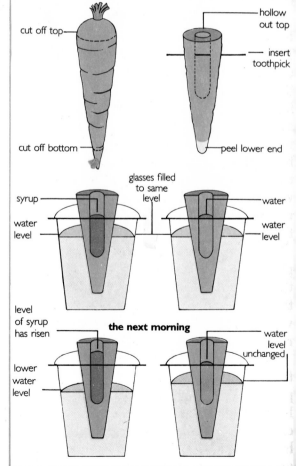

▶ You can do your own experiment to show how osmosis works. First peel two large carrots and cut off their ends. Starting at the larger end, hollow out each carrot with a corkscrew or apple corer, without splitting the carrot. Fill one half full of water, and the other half full of a sugar and water syrup. Stand the carrots in two glasses of water, up to the level of the liquids inside the carrots. Then wait for a day or so, and look at the levels. In the carrot with the syrup, the liquid will have risen above the level of the surrounding water due to the passage of water through the carrot into the more concentrated syrupy solution. The level of water in the other carrot should have remained the same. This is precisely how plants absorb moisture through their roots.

massive root system. A two-year-old grass plant may have a total root length, including all the root hairs, of over 483 km (300 miles)! As a plant's roots spread through the soil new root hairs are continually being formed.

Osmosis

But how do the root hairs take in water? Inside the cells of the root hairs there is a greater concentration of mineral salts than in the water in the soil. As a result water passes through the cell membrane of the root hairs into the plant in a process scientists call *osmosis*. The flow of water into the cells causes the water pressure in these cells to increase, which forces water from cell to cell, probably along the cell walls, to even out the pressure. The water eventually reaches bundles of dead cells with strengthened walls. These cells are called xylem vessels and form long microscopic tubes. It is through these tubes that water is transported throughout the plant, reaching the leaves in a network of veins in the leaf itself.

Evaporation

The main force that drives the water upwards is the *evaporation* of water from the leaf through its stomata. As water is lost from the plant into the surrounding air, water in the xylem vessels replaces it, and more water is absorbed by the root hairs. This process continues throughout the life of the plant, making its stem a water column – though it's hard to imagine the trunk of a giant redwood in this way.

Only 5 per cent of all the water that a plant takes in is used for photosynthesis, the rest is lost to the air. The pressure of the water, however, performs a second vital function: it helps to keep the plant rigid and upright as it grows.

Plants have a similar system for transporting the sugars and starches produced by photosynthesis in their leaves to the rest of the plant. Living cells, called phloem, are grouped into bundles laid end to end and the sugars and starches pass along them.

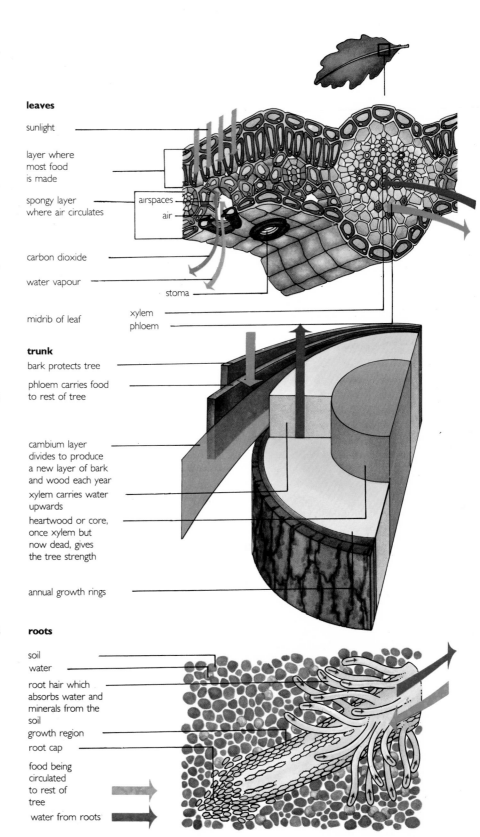

leaves
sunlight
layer where most food is made
spongy layer where air circulates
airspaces
air
carbon dioxide
water vapour
stoma
midrib of leaf
xylem
phloem

trunk
bark protects tree
phloem carries food to rest of tree
cambium layer divides to produce a new layer of bark and wood each year
xylem carries water upwards
heartwood or core, once xylem but now dead, gives the tree strength
annual growth rings

roots
soil
water
root hair which absorbs water and minerals from the soil
growth region
root cap
food being circulated to rest of tree
water from roots

▲ The diagram shows the three main stages of the movement of water through a tree from roots to leaves. It also shows how food made in the leaves of the plant travels in the reverse direction – from the leaves down to the roots.

FLOWERS

Flowers are so beautiful and give us so much enjoyment, whether in the countryside, in the garden, or decorating our homes, that it is easy to forget that their colour and perfume serve entirely practical purposes. They are devices to attract animals, especially insects. By visiting flowers insects spread pollen from one plant to another, and in this way ensure the plants' reproduction.

Flower structure

Flowers are complicated structures made up of different parts. If you look carefully at these parts you will see that they are often arranged in a circle. On the very outside of a typical flower are green leaf-like sepals. These protect the flower bud from frost, drying out and insect damage. In a flower such as the poppy, the sepals drop off before the flower opens. The tomato, on the other hand, retains its sepals. They are the 'star' at the end of the stalk from which each tomato hangs.

Within the ring of sepals are the petals,

often brightly coloured. Normally there are the same number of petals as sepals – from three to six. Many flowers have parts of their petals modified near the base to form nectaries – groups of cells which produce a sweet sugary substance called nectar which forms the basis of honey.

In some flowers, especially those of the monocotyledons, the sepals and petals look the same. In others, for example, anemones, the lovely colourful 'petals' are, in fact, the sepals!

Some flowers that are pollinated by the wind or water have no petals. They have no need to advertise themselves to attract pollinating insects. Grasses are a good example of plants without petals. Many trees also have small greenish, petalless flowers.

Male and female parts

Both sepals and petals enclose the flower's male and female sex organs. Most flowers contain both sets of organs. In some, the male and female parts are borne on different plants: for example the female holly plant is the only one to bear bright red berries.

The female parts (the *carpel*) are usually placed at the centre of the flower. The carpel is made up of three parts – the *ovary* which houses the immature fruit, above which is a stalk-like *style*, surmounted by the *stigma* which has a sticky surface to receive the pollen grains. The ovary may contain a single immature fruit, or *ovule*, such as in a cherry with a single stone, or it may contain thousands of them as is the case with many orchids. The style may be quite short as in buttercups or very long, as in the crocuses. Poppies are examples of plants without styles. Instead the stigma is arranged in radiating lines on top of the ovary.

The male parts tend to form a ring around the female ones. The male organ consists of the *stamen*, usually made up of a long stalk, the filament, which ends in the pollen-bearing structure, the *anther*. Each anther contains pollen sacs from which are produced thousands of millions

▼ These are the drawings of flowers botanists make to show their structure. The drawings on the left are slices down the flower head. Those on the right show the arrangement of the parts of the flower looking from above.

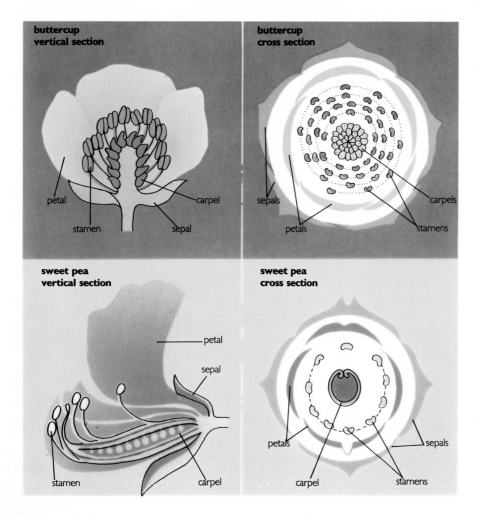

28

◄ The flowers of the snowdrop are carried singly and have two groups of three petal-like segments.

▼ When cyclamen flowers make (set) seed, the flower stem forms a spiral (left) to bring the seed to the ground.

▲ The foxglove is the source of digitalin, the first effective remedy for some forms of heart disease.

► A honey bee collects nectar from a thistle. Pollen from other thistles the bee has visited will pollinate this one.

▲ A malachite sunbird perches on a king protea, a South African plant. The bird's long bill is well adapted for reaching the flower's plentiful nectar.

of pollen grains. The pollen grains contain the male sex cells.

Under a microscope the pollen grains from different plants look quite different from one another. They may be round, star-shaped, pitted or warty-looking. These pollen grains can tell us a lot about what kind of vegetation was on Earth thousands, or even millions, of years ago,

for a good deal of pollen has been preserved, especially in the peat of bogs. By looking closely at the variety of pollen grains found in different layers of peat, we can gain a good picture of what plants were growing at different times.

Flower arrangement and colour
The wonderful thing about flowers is the

variety of their colours, shapes and forms. Some are simple like a tulip, with one flower on one stalk. But a large number of plants have many flowers arranged together; this arrangement is called an inflorescence. The white 'umbrellas' of hogweed and angelica have flowers like this. Daisies are complex inflorescences composed of different kinds of flowers on a single flower head. The outer white ray florets of a daisy serve to attract insects while the yellow disc florets have reduced petals and contain the reproductive parts.

The colours of flowers are produced by pigments, either contained in special structures called plastids, inside the cell, or distributed throughout the cell. White flowers have no pigment at all – their whiteness is due to the reflection of light from very many tiny air spaces.

POLLINATION

When you see a bee buzzing around a flower, it is looking for nectar. This endless search for food makes bees important in the *pollination* of flowers.

As an insect enters a flower its body brushes up against the flower's anthers and pollen grains get dislodged and stick to the insect's body. When the insect visits another flower of the same kind, these pollen grains get scraped on to the stigma – the female part of the flower. In this way the flower is pollinated.

The next stage is for the pollen grains, containing the male sex cells, to unite with the female sex cell, the ovule. This process is called fertilization. It results in the ovule developing into a seed which the plant releases, and from which a new young plant grows in the next season.

Bees are just one of many different kinds of insects that visit flowers. Over 80 per cent of all flowers are pollinated by insects, and flowers and insects depend on each other to survive. Flowers show some marvellous ways of attracting their insect guests, mainly by colour and scent. For example some flowers smell of rotten meat to attract flies which carry off their pollen grains. Flowers that open up at night, or release their perfume at this time, are often light-coloured and show up well in the dark. Plants such as honeysuckle and evening primrose are pollinated by night-flying moths.

Insects may not see the same colours as us. Honeybees, for example, cannot see reds or oranges. You will find that most flowers with insect visitors are yellow, purple or pinkish-mauve. Some petals have guide lines on them (often invisible to our eyes), to direct the insects to the nectar source.

Orchids show some of the most amazing devices to attract insects. In many cases the insects remove the whole stamen which they carry on to the next plant. Some orchid flowers, such as the bee, wasp and fly orchids, actually resemble insects. Here, pollination is effected by the male insect actually trying to mate with the flower which, because of its colour and smell, he takes to be a female insect.

In the tropics, large red flowers such as hibiscus are pollinated by birds because they can see this colour particularly well. Hummingbirds are common pollinators of flowers in North and South America.

Some mammals, for example bats, pollinate flowers. They visit the large blooms of the banana tree and the giant saguaro cactus. In Australia, a small honey possum pollinates flowers such as banksias with its long tongue.

Wind pollination

Most of the remaining 20 per cent or so of flowering plants are pollinated by the wind. One grass plant can release over 200 million very small light pollen

▼ Male catkins of the silver birch tree scattering pollen as they are blown by the wind.

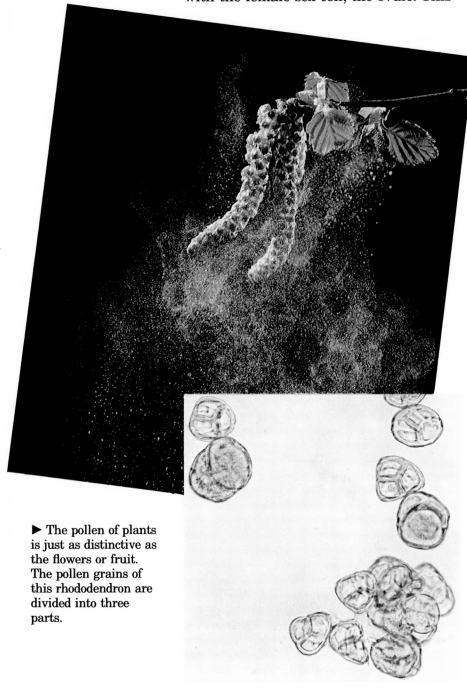

▶ The pollen of plants is just as distinctive as the flowers or fruit. The pollen grains of this rhododendron are divided into three parts.

32

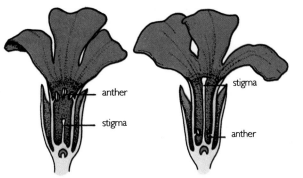

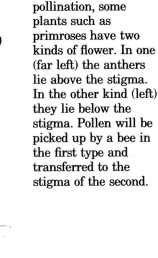

◀ To ensure cross-pollination, some plants such as primroses have two kinds of flower. In one (far left) the anthers lie above the stigma. In the other kind (left) they lie below the stigma. Pollen will be picked up by a bee in the first type and transferred to the stigma of the second.

grains. Of course not many of these find female plants and the wastage is enormous. Grass pollen is one of the main causes of hay fever from which many people suffer in summer. Many trees are also wind-pollinated.

Cross-pollination

When an insect carries, or the wind blows, pollen from one plant to another it is called cross-pollination. The advantage of cross-pollination is that you get a variety of plants adapted for slightly different conditions. For example, if one year there is a drought, some seeds that are produced will be able to adapt better to this change in conditions and they will survive.

Self-pollination

But, of course, there is no guarantee that a particular insect will find another flower of the same kind, or that wind-blown pollen will either. Because of this uncertainty some flowers pollinate themselves. This self-pollination ensures fertilization, but does not give the variety that cross-fertilization achieves. Some flowers use a mixture of both methods. Violets, for instance, produce insect-pollinated spring flowers, but they also produce later green flowers that are self-pollinating.

Pollination is a fascinating process that has evolved over millions of years. Next time you see an insect on a flower, take a closer look and try to find out how that insect is pollinating that particular plant.

◀ A slender-tailed hunting wasp is the pollinating agent of this flower. As it sucks up nectar from the flower, its head brushes against the flower's anthers and picks up sticky pollen grains. Some of these get rubbed off when the wasp visits the flowers of another plant.

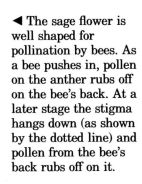

◀ The sage flower is well shaped for pollination by bees. As a bee pushes in, pollen on the anther rubs off on the bee's back. At a later stage the stigma hangs down (as shown by the dotted line) and pollen from the bee's back rubs off on it.

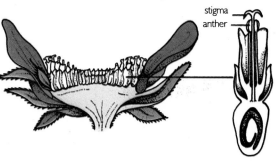

◀ Flowers of the daisy family, for example the sunflower, are made up of many florets (see detail). Mature stigmas that do not receive pollen by cross-pollination curl back to be self-pollinated by their own anthers.

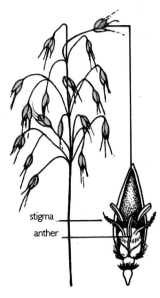

◀ Many grasses are wind-pollinated. Their anthers and stigmas hang out of the small flowers or florets (see detail). Anthers dangle loosely and the light pollen is easily blown by the wind. Stigmas are feathery to enable them to trap pollen from the air.

THE LIFE CYCLE ENDS – AND BEGINS

The production of seeds is the final stage in the life of a flowering plant; at the same time it marks the beginning of a new generation of plants.

Seeds

Once fertilized, the ovule develops rapidly into a seed. The part of the seed that will become the new plant is called the embryo. It is made up of the *plumule* (the leaf part) and the *radicle* (the root part). The remainder consists of a food store called the *endosperm* whose function is to nourish the seed once it starts to germinate. Wheat and rice are good examples of seeds with well-developed endosperms which provide food for people. Beans and peas, however, have only a small endosperm. Their food reserves are stored inside the fat seed leaves.

Fruits

While the seed is developing, other parts of the flower, especially the remaining female parts, are developing into fruits. It is a complicated process as some parts shrivel and die while other parts swell and fuse together.

A pea pod is actually the fruit of the pea plant, and the peas it contains are the seeds. The strawberry 'fruit' is not a

▲ The seed heads of the dandelion are made up of many small seeds with their own parachute of hairs which helps the wind carry them to a new place to grow.

▼ The real fruits of a strawberry are the pale seeds that are embedded in a fleshy structure called the receptacle. Birds, and insects such as wasps, will eat strawberries and other soft fruits.

▲ The raspberry is made up of many individual fruits clustered together.

real fruit at all. It consists of the swollen flower base in which are embedded many tiny individual fruits. An apple consists of a swollen ovary, the apple core, surrounded by the swollen base of the flower which is the part of the apple that we eat.

Seed dispersal

New seeds have a better chance of surviving if they settle away from the parent plant, where they will not be competing for food and light with a strong, well-established plant. There are many ways in which plants achieve this. Members of the pea family, such as gorse, have 'explosive fruits'. As their seed pods dry out they twist and curl back, flicking out the fruit.

Dispersal by wind is common. Poppies and snapdragons use a 'saltshaker' method. The ripe ovaries form a dry hollow capsule with many tiny seeds. As the plants sway in the wind the seeds are scattered from small openings in the seed capsules. Thistles, willow herb and dandelion all have light feathery seeds which are carried like miniature parachutes by the wind. Many trees, for example ash, sycamore and lime, have winged seeds which slow the fall of the fruits and make them spin away from the parent tree.

Animals also play an important part in dispersing seeds. Burdock and goosegrass are just two of many plants whose seeds are covered in tiny hooks which attach themselves to the fur of mammals. Foxes and other mammals eat juicy woodland fruits. Blackberries are eaten by both mammals and birds. As the fruits are digested the seeds pass untouched through the animals' digestive systems and, in the process, are carried long distances from the original plant. In the autumn birds consume many berries, the fleshy parts of which provide them with nourishment, but the seeds themselves are not digested and again often end up many miles from where the birds ate the fruit.

▼ Burdock seeds have small hooks which catch on to the fur of any animal that brushes past the plant. With luck, the 'burr' will fall off the animal far from the parent plant.

▲ The bright berries of the yew are attractive to birds who eat the fleshy fruit, so helping the dispersal of the tree's seeds.

▲ The seeds of the maple have wings which help the seeds glide some distance away from the parent tree.

▶ The berries of the Chinese lantern are protected by an orange 'paper lantern' which withers when the berries ripen.

3 PLANTS WE DEPEND UPON

◄ A germinating grain of maize shows how the stem grows upwards towards the light and the root grows downwards into the soil. This will always happen in a plant, even if the seed has been planted upside down.

THE PRODUCTIVE GRASSES

There are about 10,000 different kinds of grass, which range from the short turf plants that make up our lawns to giant bamboos 35 m (120 ft) high. The seeds of various grasses such as wheat, barley, maize and rice feed millions of people every year.

Grasses are found all over the world and in some places cover huge areas of open country. Well over 1,300 million hectares (3,200 million acres) of the Earth's surface is covered by grasses. The main grassland regions include the prairies of North America (though much is now farmland), the pampas of South America, the savanna of Africa and the steppes of Central Asia. These grasslands support vast herds of cattle which feed on the grasses and also large numbers of wild animals. The African savanna, in particular, is tremendously rich in wildlife. It supports a great variety of plant-eating animals such as antelope, zebra and wildebeest, as well as the animals, such as lions, hunting dogs and jackals, that prey on them.

All grasses have smooth, shiny, usually hollow stems, with regularly spaced joints. A leaf grows out from each joint and is enclosed at its base by a protective sheath. The leaf itself is long and narrow and the veins run parallel to each other. Grasses have small flowers which grow out from the top of the stem. The flowers are carried in groups called spikelets. Grass plants usually carry both male and female flowers. The wind carries the pollen grains to different grass plants, just when the female flowers are ready to receive the maximum amount. For example in a field of rye, thousands of male flowers open at the same time, releasing a cloud of pollen which drifts on to the open female flowers. All this happens in a matter of minutes and can happen several times in one day.

Grasses can also multiply by means of underground stems called stolons, or stems called runners that trail over the ground.

Cereals
Of all cereal crops, wheat is certainly the most important. It was cultivated as long as 5,000 years ago in the warm climate of Egypt, although now wheat can be grown in places where the summers are hot and dry and the winters are cold and wet. North America, the Soviet Union and Europe produce most of the world's wheat. The seeds of wheat are ground

▼ Today wheat growing is big business. Massive combine harvesters collect and process the crop, doing the work of many men. The harvest here is in one of the many wheat growing areas of North America known as the 'bread basket'.

into flour to make the bread we eat. Wheat also forms the basis of many breakfast cereals.

Oats are another kind of cereal. They are grown in regions such as Scandinavia where the summers are short. Oatmeal and porridge are perhaps the best-known human foods made from oats, which are also an important animal food.

Rye, another cereal, is grown mainly on the light sandy soils of Central Europe. It is used to make a dark, tasty bread. Barley is used to make malt which is used in beer making.

Sorghum and millet are cereals that are grown in tropical countries.

Maize

One grass that looks quite different from other kinds is maize or corn. We can eat the juicy seed heads as corn-on-the-cob or as popcorn. But corn has very many other uses – it is ground into flour, made into starch and used to make sweet syrups. Chickens are fed on the dried seed heads and cattle eat the leaves. The sheaths surrounding the seed heads are used for making paper and in many parts of South America the stalks are used as a building material for walls and roofs. Maize was first cultivated from the wild varieties by the South American Indians, 7,000 years ago. Today the world's main producer is the United States.

Rice

Rice provides food for half the world's population. This important food plant probably once grew wild as a swamp grass. Today, over 2,000 varieties of rice exist, so that the crop can be cultivated in a wide range of soils and climates. In many parts of the world, such as south-east Asia, rice is the basic food. As puffed rice we may eat it as a breakfast cereal, and it is also made into cakes and puddings and is used to make a fine paper.

Rice grows best in tropical and subtropical countries where it is warm and wet. The rice seeds are first sown in wet ground. After 25–50 days the young plants are transplanted into 'paddies'. These are flat fields that can be flooded with water to a depth of 10–20 cm (4–8 in). Paddies are often surrounded by low earth walls to keep the water in. About six months after the rice is planted

▲ A selection of different grasses shows how the seeds are borne in bundles at the end of the stem. Cultivated grasses such as maize and wheat have all been developed from wild varieties. Bamboos are long-living grasses, and flower at very irregular intervals, but when they do flower, all the plants of the same type flower at the same time and then they die.

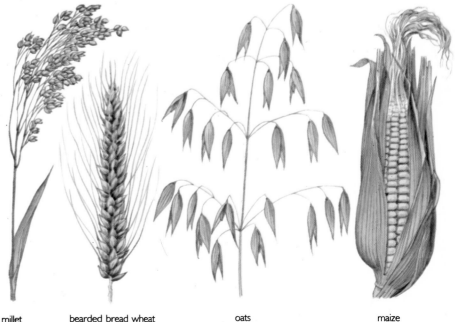

bamboo   sugar cane   rice   millet   bearded bread wheat   oats   maize

▲ Rice plants need water to mature. Here young rice plants are being transplanted into a flooded field in Java. The seedlings are placed in groups of two to five plants.

▲ Sugar beet is a relative of beetroot. Cultivation of the sugar beet started in northern Germany about 175 years ago, and it is now nearly as important a source of sugar as sugar cane.

in the paddy fields, it develops seeds. Once the seeds are ripe, the paddies are drained and the rice is cut by hand with knives and sickles. Bundles of rice are stacked in the sun to dry, then the seeds are separated from the plant by threshing, either by animals that trample the plants, or by machines.

The threshed rice is known as rough or paddy rice because it is still covered with rough husks. These are removed by grinding the rice in a mill, or simply by pounding it on a stone. The rice grains at this stage have a brown skin called bran which is nutritious as it contains oil, protein, minerals and vitamins. The only problem is that rice does not keep long in this state, so it is cleaned and polished. Unfortunately this process removes the nutrients, leaving mainly starch. People who exist chiefly on this polished rice can develop a disease called beriberi which affects the nervous system.

Sugar cane

A grass prized for its sweet juice since ancient times is sugar cane. Two-thirds of all the sugar we eat comes from this plant. It grows wild in India and the Pacific Ocean islands, but most cultivated sugar cane now comes from India and Cuba.

Sugar cane is one of the largest of the grasses. It takes only a year to grow to a height of 4–5 m (13–16 ft). When the plant is mature it has stout solid stems which are crushed to extract the sugar. Sugar cane is unusual because it seldom flowers and produces good seeds. To get a new crop of sugar cane, some of the stalks are laid in deep furrows in the soil. Shoots grow from the joints of these stalks. These new plants produce sugar cane after 18–30 months.

After harvesting, the sugar cane is taken to a mill to be cleaned. It is then crushed between large steel rollers. The juice is strained and made into a syrup by boiling much of the liquid away. The sugar crystals that form are refined still further until pure sugar crystals are produced.

Molasses is a thick dark syrup which is drained from the cane. Molasses is used to sweeten candies and gingerbread. Some of it is used as animal feed, some for making rum.

The dry parts of the cane left after it has been crushed and all the juice extracted is called bagasse. It is used to make many things, including plastics and paper.

Sugar beet

Sugar beet, the other common plant source of sugar, is grown in northern countries. But in this plant it is the swollen root, not the stem, that is used to produce sugar.

▶ Cutting sugar cane
in Guadeloupe, an
island in the West
Indies.

VEGETABLES

▲ Carrots are one of many root vegetables that we eat. The orange type that is most commonly grown originated in Afghanistan, although there are also purple and white kinds.

▲ One potato plant can yield many pounds of potatoes. Today, hundreds of varieties of potato have been developed from the little wild species that grew in the Andes of South America.

The plants that we call vegetables are a very important part of our diet. They provide us with the vitamins and minerals essential for good health. Our vegetables come from all parts of plants, from the roots to the seeds.

Underground roots and stems
Think of the vegetables that you eat – or are made to eat! Many come from those parts of a plant that grow below ground. The carrot, for example, was developed, like many of our vegetables, from a weedy-looking wild plant. The thick root of the carrot is the part we eat and young carrots can taste remarkably sweet. Carrots are particularly rich in vitamin A, which is necessary for healthy eyesight. Vitamin A is also important for a healthy skin and helps babies and children grow properly.

Beetroots, turnips, parsnips and swedes are also underground roots. In eastern Europe and the Soviet Union, where many green vegetables are difficult to grow because of the long cold winters, these root vegetables form an important part of the diet. Beetroot is made into a delicious soup called borscht. Parsnips can be made into a drink like coffee and are sometimes made into wine. Swedes and turnips provide an alternative source of vitamin C for those people who cannot get green vegetables or citrus fruits.

The popular potato
Everyone knows what a potato looks and tastes like. There are hundreds of ways to cook this vegetable. It came originally from the high Andes of South America and was brought to Europe in the sixteenth century. The part of the potato that we eat, the tuber, is really an underground stem. It is rich in starch and some vitamins.

Potatoes keep well if protected from the cold, which made them an important winter food in northern and central Europe in the days before foods could be canned and frozen to keep them fresh.

New kinds of potato are developed from the seeds produced by the potato flower, new crops of potatoes are grown from the potatoes themselves. 'Seed' potatoes are planted in the spring and the new potato plants grow from the 'eyes' of the old potato. The new plants feed on the starch stored in the potato until they have produced green shoots above ground and

▲ All parts of the fennel plant have a strong aniseed flavour. The swollen rootstock shown here makes a delicious vegetable hot or cold.

▼ Asparagus has been a delicacy since Roman times. We only eat the tender young shoots. If these are not picked they develop into lovely delicate green fronds.

▲ Onions growing (**top right**) and an onion cut down the middle (**above**). The edible part is actually formed from thick leaf bases which grow from the shortened stem at the bottom of the bulb.

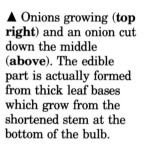

► Garlic is related to the onion but has a stronger flavour. It is used for seasoning food and is grown in countries around the Mediterranean.

can make their own food by means of photosynthesis.

In 1845 a disease called potato blight killed the European potato crop. Thousands of people starved to death. Because of this famine, many Irish people emigrated to America to start a new life.

Other vegetables

Apart from underground bulbs, roots and stems, we eat various parts of other plants. For example, we eat the leaves of lettuce and cabbage, the young flowers of cauliflower and broccoli, the leaf stalks of celery, the young shoots of asparagus and

the seeds of peas and beans.

All these vegetables provide us with an important source of minerals and vitamins which we need to grow strong and healthy. In fact, doctors have discovered that in areas of the world where there are many diseases caused by poor nutrition, Vitamin A deficiency can be cured if patients eat a few leaves of a green vegetable each day.

Green vegetables also give us roughage. They contain a lot of material called cellulose which cannot be digested, but that helps the movement of food along the digestive system.

▲ The asparagus plant has extremely fibrous roots growing from the base of the plant's stems.

LEGUMES

Peas, beans and peanuts are edible examples of the plants known as legumes. Other legumes, such as broom, lupins and, of course, the sweet pea, are grown for their attractive flowers. In all, there are some 14,000 different kinds of legumes. Almost all of them produce pods that enclose the seeds.

Important food plants

Edible legumes, many of which we also call vegetables, have been an important part of people's diet for thousands of years. Long before the great Inca civilization of Peru, several thousand years ago, people in that country were eating kidney beans. In fact many kinds of beans come from South America, including the scarlet runner bean. This plant was introduced into Britain in 1633 where it was first grown as an ornamental garden plant for its scarlet red flowers. It was not until the eighteenth century that it was grown for its beans. Peas are probably the most popular legume in the western world. They came originally from the Mediterranean area and Afghanistan.

Apart from those legumes which are eaten when they are green and moist, many others are dried. They include lentils, used for making soups and sometimes ground into flour, and the small white mung bean which is eaten throughout much of India. The freshly germinated seeds of this bean are the bean sprouts so popular in Chinese cooking.

▲ These three pictures show the germination of a kidney bean plant. The plant gets its name from its kidney-shaped leaves.

▼ Some of the many different cultivated beans. From left to right: rose coco beans, broad beans, red milch, haricot, gunga peas, flageolets, chick peas, black beans, aduki beans, soy beans, butter beans, borlotti, black-eyed, lima, bean shoots, Dutch brown. In the front are some fresh green beans.

► Peas are popular and easy to grow garden plants. They are best picked before they are fully ripe, when they are green and moist.

The peanut is unusual as its pods do not burst open to shed their seeds. The flower stalks that bear the developing pods grow down into the ground, where the pods ripen. Peanuts are rich in fats and oils. Apart from roasted nuts and peanut butter, they are used to make cooking oil, and in the manufacture of soap and diesel fuels. Large-scale peanut growing is carried out in China, India, West Africa and the southern United States.

Beans instead of meat

Legumes are rich in protein, which many people in western countries get from eating meat, fish, eggs and cheese. The soyabean is especially rich in protein. It came originally from China. Although it was not introduced to the West until the early nineteenth century, it is now widely grown. It is also cultivated for its oil and as an animal feed. Vast areas of marshes in the state of Louisiana in the United States have been drained to grow this important crop. Much of it is exported to countries where meat protein is scarce.

Natural fertilizers

Apart from their value as food, legumes are also useful because they act as natural fertilizers and enrich the soil. Certain bacteria in the soil, called nitrogen-fixing bacteria, enter the roots of legumes. There they produce substances called nitrates which contain nitrogen, which is essential for the healthy growth of all plants. Legumes such as lucerne or alfalfa are often grown in large fields and ploughed back into the soil to make way for other plants the following year. Lucerne is also an important feed plant for cattle.

Legumes have many other uses. The carob tree is grown round the Mediterranean for its gum, used in foods and certain industrial products. Acacia trees are a rich source of nectar from which bees make a delicious honey.

FOOD FROM THE TROPICS

Many of the common household drinks such as tea, coffee and cocoa come from plants that grow in warm, often tropical countries. Most are now grown over a much wider area than they occur naturally. In the countries where they are cultivated, these crops represent an important source of income to the local people.

Cocoa and chocolate

The cacao tree grows wild in the tropical forests of South America, and was grown by the Aztecs in Mexico long before America was discovered by Europeans.

Though the tree grows to 13 m (40 ft) or more, it is usually pruned to about 6 m (20 ft) to make harvesting easier. The tree sprouts tiny pink blossoms on the old wood of the trunk and larger branches. These flowers develop into fleshy pods, up to 25.5 cm (10 in) long. The pods are brightly coloured, yellow, orange, red or purple. Each pod contains about 30 whitish seeds or 'beans'. When the seeds are ripe, the shell of the pod is crushed and the seeds are removed and fermented in vats to develop the chocolate flavour. At this stage the beans are exported to the countries where the chocolate is to be made. The beans are first roasted and then ground. After that sugar, vanilla and other ingredients are added. Different chocolate makers have secret recipes to improve the taste and quality of the chocolate they make.

Today some cacao beans come from South America, but most are grown in West Africa. Venezuela produces the best-quality beans.

Coffee

The reverse is true of the coffee plant, for it came from Africa but is now mainly grown in South America, especially in the tropical highlands of Brazil. The plant is

▼ Each ripe red berry of the coffee plant contains two beans.

▼ After the coffee beans are removed they are washed and laid out in the sun to dry. The drying process may take two weeks. Here, in Colombia, the beans are being turned to make sure they are thoroughly dried.

▲ The pawpaw is a quick-growing tropical tree which has succulent fruit.

▲ The cacao tree has large, drooping, leathery leaves. On this one, the pods have developed on the main trunk.

▼ Coconuts cut open reveal the white flesh and the matted husk. All parts of the coconut are useful.

a *shrub* with glossy green leaves and bears fragrant white flowers two or three times a year. The flowers give rise to berries which contain two seeds or beans. The berries are picked, the beans are removed from their shells, dried and then roasted to bring out the strong coffee aroma. The longer the beans are roasted, the darker they become and the stronger the taste of the coffee.

Coffee contains a substance called caffeine, which is also found in tea, cocoa and cola drinks. Caffeine stimulates the nervous system. It makes people feel more awake and helps them overcome tiredness, but its effect does not last very long. If you drink too much coffee it can make you feel restless or prevent you getting to sleep easily.

The coconut palm, a tree of plenty

The coconut is the fruit of the coconut palm, a tall tree that grows in tropical countries by the sea. No one knows where this plant originally came from because it is so widely spread. One of these palm trees can produce about 50 coconuts a year. They fall off the tree naturally and, because they float well, they have travelled many hundreds of miles on

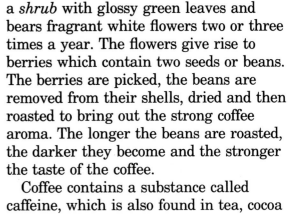

▲ Coconut palms growing on a tropical beach. Apart from the coconuts, the tree supplies building material from the trunks and the leaves provide thatch for roofs.

◄ Bananas grow on a long stalk which keeps growing longer. This produces clusters of yellow flowers. Their bracts drop off and the fruits develop into 'hands' of 10 to 20 bananas. The beautiful purple part of the flower remains at the end of the stem. The different types of bananas, or plantains, are staple foods in tropical countries. Bananas are also an important export for countries such as Ecuador and the islands of the West Indies.

▲ The pineapple appears to be one large fruit, but it is actually made up of many small juicy fruits joined together. Besides the fruit, the pineapple leaves have fibres that are sometimes made into cloth, yarn or cord.

ocean currents, to settle and grow in new areas.

The white coconut flesh that we eat is only one part of this useful fruit. Inside the fruit is a delicious 'milk', which is really there to nourish the seedling coconut when it first sprouts on some dry salty beach.

The inner part of the coconut is lined with a hard, oily flesh. This flesh is known as copra when it is dried. It is used to make soap, candles and margarine. The fibrous outer husk of the coconut, known as coir, produces a strong and hard-wearing fibre, from which ropes, mats and baskets are made. All these useful products from one kind of tree make the coconut palm extremely important in the regions where it grows.

Other crops from the tropics
Bananas, pineapples, mangoes and papayas are a few of the tropical fruits that are now grown in large plantations mainly to feed people who live thousands of miles away.

The pineapple comes from South America, although today most pineapples are grown in Hawaii, where the climate is warm and wet. After fruiting, a new pineapple plant can be grown only from the crown of leaves at the top of the fruit. You can try growing a pineapple yourself. Cut the top off, place it in a shallow dish of water and wait for the roots to form. Then put it in a pot with good rich earth and keep it warm. If nothing happens, cover it with a plastic bag, as this acts like a miniature greenhouse, keeping in both the heat and moisture. Once the plant roots it will grow into a bushy plant. It does not need a very large pot. It's not so easy to get it to produce fruit. If you don't live in a warm climate, you need a really warm greenhouse or warm, sunny spot in the house – and patience!

45

THE FRUIT OF THE VINE

Grapes are the fruit of a plant called a vine. These are plants that have clinging tendrils and are related to the Virginia creeper which is grown to cover fences and walls. There are some 5,000 different kinds of vine that produce grapes. Some vines are grown for the fruit alone, while many others are cultivated for grapes that will be made into wine.

Grape vines are one of the oldest cultivated plants. They came originally from the area around the Black and Caspian seas, but are now grown in many countries, including Germany, France, Italy, Spain, the United States and Australia.

Wine

Growing grapes for wine is a very ancient practice. Looking after or tending vine plants is very complicated because the plants must be pruned at the right time, fed with fertilizer, tied up to prevent the grapes dragging on the ground, and above all the vines must be protected against bad weather. During May there may be late frosts that could damage the plants. To prevent this, people sit up all night to fuel stoves that warm the air. As grapes ripen the outer skin becomes covered with a whitish 'bloom'. This is actually a fungus called yeast which plays an important part in wine-making. It ferments the grapes' sugars to make alcohol.

In 1870 a small plant bug called phylloxera killed off most of the vines in France and the rest of Europe. This was a disaster for the wine-growers so new vines had to be *grafted* from American plants and it took many years for the harvest to recover.

Apart from wine, grapes are grown for raisins, currants and sultanas, which are dried red or green grapes. Centuries ago, before sugar was as common as it is today, these dried fruits were highly prized as sweeteners. Today, California produces the most raisin grapes.

▼ Grape vines will grow on a variety of soils but grapes need hot sun to develop and ripen. You can see the white bloom of yeast on these bunches of ripe grapes.

CITRUS FRUITS

◄ The orange harvest in Sicily. Citrus fruits are one of the main exports of this Italian island.

Citrus fruits include oranges, lemons and grapefruit. We eat a lot of them but, like many fruits we take for granted today, they are a relatively recent addition to our diet. Citrus fruits all grow on evergreen trees. The fruits develop from fragrant white or pink blossoms. Sometimes the blossoms are collected to make perfume.

The orange came originally from China. It has been grown there for thousands of years. The oranges we eat today, like most of the other fruits and vegetables, are the result of careful crossbreeding of different varieties. Blood oranges have red juice while others, like the Jaffa orange, have no pips. Oranges are grown today on a big scale in warm countries such as Spain and Italy. Florida and California in the United States also have very large orange groves.

The lemon is also a plant from the East, introduced to many other parts of the world. Lemons are picked when they are still green and are stored until they turn a beautiful waxy yellow. Limes are like small green lemons. They are grown mainly in Mexico and the West Indies.

The grapefruit is the most recent of citrus fruits. It arose in the West Indies in the eighteenth century, a hybrid of the sweet orange and a fruit called a shaddock that was introduced into the West Indies in the seventeenth century.

Apart from being good to eat, juicy and refreshing, citrus fruits are an important source of vitamin C, one of the vitamins vital for good health. You can also get this vitamin from eating fresh vegetables. A lack of vitamin C causes a disease called scurvy which affects the skin and gums. Sailors in the olden days used to suffer from it particularly badly because on long voyages they had no means of keeping a supply of fresh fruit and vegetables on board their ships.

DRUGS AND POISONS

► The beautiful opium poppy is grown in the Middle East for its seed heads from which the drugs codeine and morphine are extracted. The dried seeds are also used to flavour food.

The Sumerians who lived in Mesopotamia (in much the area of modern Iraq) over 5,000 years ago used plants as medicine. We know this because archeologists have found clay tablets with prescriptions for medicines on them, but sadly we do not know what disease or illness the medicines were supposed to cure. However, plant medicines have been used all over the world since then. There is much evidence from, for example, ancient China, Egypt and Greece, telling us how plants were used to cure illnesses of all kinds. Many of these plants are used in modern medicines. Take for example the drug opium, extracted from the juices of the seed head of the opium poppy. This substance was known to the Greeks as an effective painkiller. Today, the drug codeine is extracted from the poppy and widely used for the relief of pain. It is much safer than opium and morphine, which also comes from the opium poppy.

The Greeks also knew the drug belladonna, which comes from the plant known as deadly nightshade. The fruits of this plant are extremely poisonous, but small doses of the drug are used to treat upset stomachs. It is also useful in ophthalmology because eye drops made from it will enlarge the pupil.

In fact, many drugs we use today came from plants. Aspirin, probably the most common pain-reliever, was originally made from the bark of willow trees. Even more important is penicillin, made from a microscopic fungus. This drug is now widely prescribed to treat many bacterial infections. Because of the great demand for them, drugs are now manufactured artificially on a big scale.

Folk medicine
People living in country areas have always used plants as drugs, aids to digestion and as herbs to flavour their foods. A herbal tea made from the leaves of the foxglove was known to help dropsy. This is a condition where parts of the body swell up with fluid, and is often caused by heart disease. Digitalin, a substance extracted from the foxglove, was one of the first effective drugs for heart disease. And modern medicine still uses an extract of this plant for heart conditions. There are many examples of such plants. Herbal teas are still popular for less serious complaints. One tea, made from the flowers of the small wild plant chamomile, a kind of daisy, is taken by people to help them sleep better. Generally, it works very well, although some folk medicines are not so reliable.

Poisons
As already mentioned, some of the plants from which we get drugs can be extremely dangerous if used incorrectly. Many plants have parts that are poisonous. Some of these are very common wild plants and others we even grow in our gardens. For example, it is extremely dangerous to eat the leaves of the rhubarb plant, because they contain a substance called oxalic acid. However, the stems, the parts we eat, are quite harmless. The seeds of the laburnum tree, a tree with attractive yellow blossoms, are also poisonous. Each year many children end up in hospital from eating them – attracted by what look like clusters of miniature pea pods. The berries of the holly used in many countries as a Christmas decoration are also harmful if eaten. So, be careful of any plant you are not sure about.

▶ The foxglove is found both in the wild and cultivated in gardens. The drug digitalin, which is obtained from the plant, slows the heart and is useful in many heart-related diseases.

▼ The colourful fly agaric fungus is poisonous and if eaten can cause blindness and hallucinations. The ancient Vikings used to eat parts of this fungus before they went on raids. It made them feel both mad and brave.

▲ Deadly nightshade, as its name suggests, is very poisonous. The berries change from green to black and are about the size of cherries.

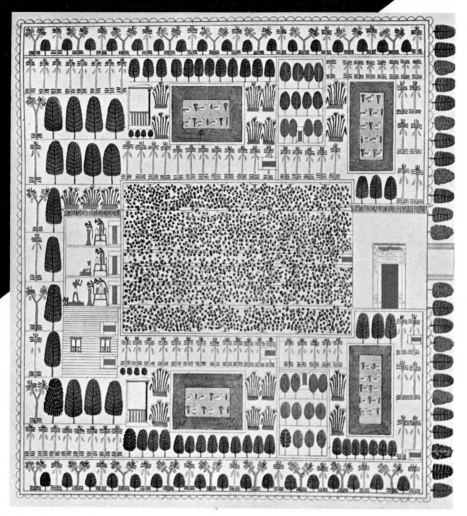

▲ Gardens are not new, although originally they belonged only to the richest and most aristocratic members of society. This plan for a formal garden comes from Ancient Egypt.

Flowers have been grown for decoration for over 3,000 years although, as far as we know, the earliest gardens were used to grow only herbs and other useful plants. The first real gardens, symmetrically arranged with walls, trees and pools, were made in ancient Egypt about 1500 BC, and soon included plants grown for their beauty and not just their usefulness. The Assyrians and Babylonians to the east, in much the region of modern Iraq, made great tree parks and built artificial hills – the 'hanging gardens' of Babylon. The Chinese had pleasure gardens by the fourth century BC, and they deliberately developed such flowers as chrysanthemums and tree peonies as objects of beauty. In more recent centuries flowers were grown for pleasure in ancient Rome, by the Aztecs in South America, by the Japanese and the Polynesians.

At first growing flowers and trees for ornamental purposes was a luxury for

rulers and the very rich; if the poor grew anything besides vegetables it was herbs to flavour their food and be used as medicines. During the Middle Ages in Europe monks in the monasteries were the main cultivators of these medicinal plants which eventually became garden flowers, including such varieties as marigolds, madonna lilies and hollyhocks.

Flowers today
Today gardening is a popular hobby throughout most of the world. So many people working in offices and factories find it refreshing to get home after work and look after their own patch of ground, however small. Even those without a garden can appreciate the flower beds in local parks, or grow houseplants indoors.

The plants we grow today came originally from many different countries. For example, the sweet pea comes from the Italian island of Sicily; it was first brought to England in 1699. The dahlia originated in Mexico, the chrysanthemum in China, and michaelmas daisies from wild North American asters. Whether we live in temperate or warm climates we have a vast choice of flowering plants for our gardens.

Plants with different life-spans
A good gardener knows how to organize his or her piece of land so that there is something in flower most of the year. In cool climates early colour is provided by daffodils, tulips and crocuses, plants bought as *bulbs* or *corms*. The Netherlands is a country famous for its spring bulbs, which are exported all over the world and are an important part of the country's trade.

Summer colour is often provided by *annual* plants that grow quickly from seed and flower for only one season. They include sweet peas, poppies and cornflowers, marigolds and petunias. Some plants, such as canterbury bells, flower only in their second year and then die: these are called *biennials*. Many summer favourites will in fact live for years, but these bedding plants, like geraniums, are tender and must be

protected from winter frosts. Garden plants which come up every year, like peonies, irises and michaelmas daisies, are called *perennials*.

Ornamental trees and shrubs

A garden is not complete without shrubs and trees, some of which, like rhododendrons, are evergreen and have leaves all year round. Many of these trees and shrubs can provide flowers, fruits and bright autumn leaves. The buddleia is a popular Chinese shrub with long white or purple flower spikes; it is often known as the 'butterfly bush' because it has honey-scented flowers to attract the insects that pollinate it.

Some people build heated greenhouses or glasshouses in which to grow flowers from warm countries which would die if left outside in winter. Orchids, for instance, with flowers of fantastic shapes and shades, can be grown with care under glass.

▶ The first true yellow cultivated roses were bred by a Frenchman in 1920. It took him 35 years.

▲ The wild rose is a plant of woodland edges of northern countries. One European kind is often known as the dog rose because the Romans thought it could cure the disease called rabies which is carried by dogs – an example of inaccurate folk medicine! This and other wild varieties are the ancestors of the cultivated rose.

◀ A Japanese water garden with foliage and sculpture reflected in the water has an air of tranquillity – an essential ingredient in this type of garden.

CACTI

All cacti, with the exception of one small African group, come from North and South America. The semi-deserts of Arizona and southern California are famous for their cacti, including the giant saguaro cactus which can reach 15 m (49 ft) in height and weigh over 10 tonnes (11 tons). Further south in Mexico there are even more varieties, some only a few centimetres across. South American cacti can be found at altitudes up to the snow-line – 3,700–4,700 m (12,000–15,400 ft).

The life of cacti

A cactus consists of a swollen stem armed with spines. The spines are in fact relics of leaves which have become reduced to this state over millions of years of evolution, so as to restrict the amount of water lost by these plants which grow in arid places. The stem has taken over the functions of the leaves of other plants: that is, it carries out photosynthesis and makes food. At the same time the stem acts as a water reservoir. Inside the stem are mucilages, slimy substances which can hold large amounts of water. This water is released during periods of drought. Up to 90 per cent of the weight of a cactus is water. In the very dry deserts of Chile, cacti can live for several years without a drop of water. They look dead, but after rain, they swell to life again. Often the stem of a cactus is ribbed and knobby which helps the plant shrink when it is very dry – it's rather like the action of a concertina or an accordion.

The root system generally consists of an extensive network near the soil surface. With these roots the plant can quickly absorb as much water as possible after a light shower or a sudden downpour. Droplets of dew also form on the cactus plant itself in the early morning. They run down the plant and are absorbed by the roots.

Cactus spines protect the plant from being eaten by most desert animals although some, such as tortoises, can avoid the spines or else have such tough skins that the spines do not hurt them. Cacti that grow high up on mountains have a woolly coat of fine hairs as well as spines. This protects the cactus against freezing cold and scorching heat and helps retain water around the plant.

Cactus flowers can be extremely large and beautiful. These brilliant blossoms range through all the colours except pure blue. Flowers that open during the day are pollinated by insects or birds. At night some cacti reveal huge pale flowers that look luminescent against the dark night sky. These blooms are pollinated by moths, although the saguaro cactus is pollinated by bats.

Useful cacti

The prickly pear cactus is now cultivated for its large succulent fruits which in some parts of South America are also used to feed cattle. When a large cactus gets old, the stems become woody. Though this 'wood' is light in weight, it is strong enough to use to build houses and for fuel, in areas where there are no real trees for miles around.

Many cacti contain substances from which drugs can be made. For example,

▼ This type of prickly pear cactus is cultivated for its red fruits in parts of Mexico, and in Spain and Sicily where it has been introduced.

he massive-flowered cactus called queen of the night contains a substance used in the treatment of heart disease. A well-known Mexican cactus, peyote, contains substances which are hallucinogenic. They change the way the drug-taker sees colours and hears sounds.

Cacti in danger

The cactus family may be the most endangered of all large groups of plants. At least 72 of the 268 kinds of cacti that grow in North America are so rare they are in danger of becoming extinct. Cacti are disappearing for many reasons but mainly because they are collected as attractive house plants. They are dug up by collectors and sold for enormous profits.

Fortunately in North America you can still see magnificent cacti in certain park areas such as the Organ Pipe Cactus National Monument and Saguaro National Monument in Arizona. More parks are needed in Mexico and South America to save the fantastic variety of cacti that are found there.

▲ Mexico is famous for the variety of its cacti, including these large barrel cacti growing on a rocky hillside.

▲ This row of *Cereus* cacti was planted as a windbreak and as an impenetrable barrier, just as hedges are planted around fields in cooler countries.

◄ Saguaro cacti germinate only in the shade of other desert plants. They may live more than 200 years. They grow their first branches at about the age of 75 years.

53

CARNIVOROUS PLANTS

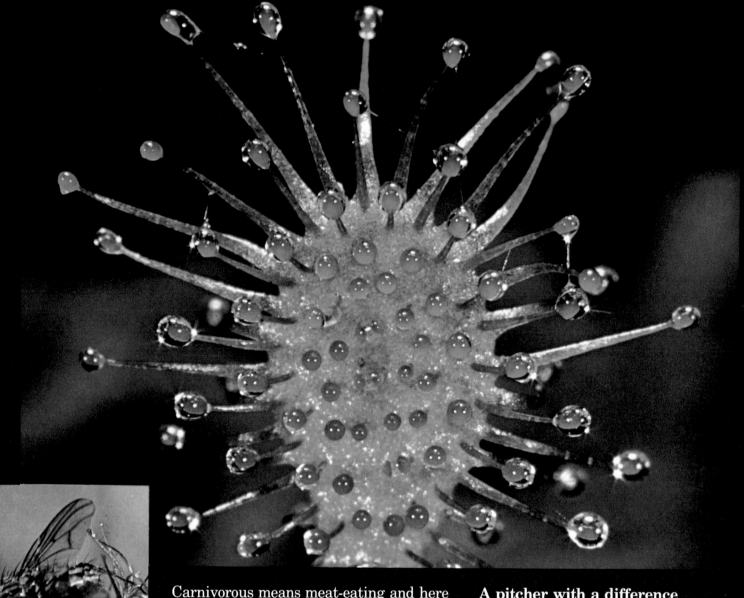

▲ One of the ribbon-leaved sundews with its prey – a large fly – that it has caught. **Top** Close-up of a sundew leaf showing the sticky glands that trap the plant's prey.

Carnivorous means meat-eating and here the term brings to mind some terrible plant monster. Fortunately, there are no plants that eat humans or even large animals, but there are some 450 different kinds of plant that capture small prey, especially insects.

Why eat insects?
Most plants obtain nourishment from minerals in the soil. Carnivorous plants tend to grow in waterlogged swamps and marshes where minerals and other substances important to plants, particularly nitrogen, are lacking. Carnivorous plants get their nitrogen from the bodies of small insects that they trap with their leaves. In this way they can live in places where other plants would die.

A pitcher with a difference
Carnivorous plants usually attract insects using some kind of lure such as smell or colour. In this way they increase their chances of catching food. The leaves of tropical pitcher plants, for example, are very efficient insect traps. Each leaf grows from a tendril, or thread-like stem. As it grows, it swells to form a colourful, lidded 'jug' or pitcher. The mouth of the pitcher has a hard and glossy rim or collar, made up of closely packed ribs. Between these, on the inside of the pitcher, are numerous nectar-secreting glands. There are also nectar glands on the lid. Insects are attracted to pitcher plants mainly by this rich nectar supply. While it crawls about on the lid, an insect such an an ant is safe. But as it searches for more nectar it reaches the rim, goes

over the edge, and once it reaches a waxy
layer below the rim, its feet can get no
grip and it soon slips down into a pool of
liquid secreted by the plant. There is also
a ring of down-pointing spine-like
growths to stop the insect climbing out.
The fluid in the pitcher contains digestive
enzymes that soon break down the body of
the insect into substances easily absorbed
by the plant. Tropical pitcher plants grow
as vines in south-east Asia but the North
American trumpet pitchers grow on the
ground and the leaves develop into
funnel-shaped tubes.

Living flypapers
The other kind of trap commonly used by
plants is the flypaper variety. Here, the
leaves have many stalked sticky glands.
Once an insect lands on a leaf it gets
stuck and the more it struggles the more
it becomes glued to the leaf. The plant
secretes digestive juices and the insect
eventually dies. There are more than 90
kinds of plants called sundews that
employ this method to capture their
insect prey. Their leaves come in all
shapes and sizes, and in some, once the
insect is snared, the leaves bend over to
aid the digestive processes.

Butterworts are small plants that grow
on wet peat. Their leaves are broad and
have a dew-like sheen from the very
many small sticky glands. Butterworts
tend to catch and digest small crawling
insects such as midges and aphids. When
an insect is trapped, the leaves slowly
curl over the prey, again to aid the
process of digesting the insect.

Spring traps
In contrast to the sundews and
butterworts, the leaves of the Venus
flytrap are like jaws that spring quickly
together trapping insects as large as
houseflies. Each leaf lobe is about 2.5 cm
(1 in) long and secretes nectar that insects
enjoy. On each lobe are three small
trigger hairs that are stimulated if an
insect lands on them, causing the jaws of
the trap to snap shut. Each trap can only
catch two or three insects during the life
of the plant. It takes from eight to ten
days for the plant to digest an insect,
after which times the valves open

leaving the insect's empty shell. The
Venus flytrap grows wild in damp sandy
soil along the coasts of North and South
Carolina in the USA.

An underwater mousetrap
Bladderworts grow in water or in wet
soils. They catch small animals in
numerous small bladders attached to
their roots. Each bladder has a one-way
entrance door, through which small
animals are sucked by the inrush of
water. The door closes and imprisons the
prey.

▼ A pitcher plant,
showing the leaf
tendrils that have
become modified to
form pitchers, or flasks
These contain a liquid
which digests any
insect that falls into
the pitcher.

▶ A Venus flytrap
about to clamp shut
and imprison a large
fly. Small trigger hairs
in the middle of each
leaf lobe cause the
leaves to close quickly.

LICHENS

If you live in a city, the chances are that you may never have seen a lichen because these plants grow best in clean air and are very sensitive to pollution. If you want to see a good range of lichens visit the coast, especially where the air is moist. Here you will find lichens that form multicoloured crusts, especially yellow, orange and black, on stone walls, old buildings and cliffs. Further inland, in moist forests, beard-like lichens hang down from trees. There are also leaf-like forms that live like mosses and cover rotten logs on the forest floor.

What are lichens?

Unique to the plant world, lichens are made up of two very different kinds of plants, an alga and a fungus, living together. This sort of relationship, in which both partners benefit, is called *symbiosis*. The alga is a green plant and manufactures its own food, some of which is taken up by the fungus. The fungus in turn provides moisture, shelter and minerals for the alga. Lichens often grow on exposed windswept rock surfaces which algae would not be able to colonize if they did not have the stronger fungus as a partner. But even so, what is interesting is that the fungus needs the alga more than the other way around. The fungus partner cannot live alone, whereas the alga can generally do so.

How lichens multiply

Lichens reproduce in several ways. The simplest method is for pieces of the plant containing both algal and fungal cells to break away. They settle and grow wherever the wind may take them. Some lichens produce special 'packets' of mixed cells called soredia, that do the same thing. Another way is for the fungus part of the lichen to produce its own spores. If such a spore does not find the right kind of algal cell to live with, it will die.

Slow-growing lichens

Lichens on rocks grow very slowly. Some lichens in the Arctic are thought to be up to 4,000 years old. As a lichen swells and shrinks, after rain and during long periods of dry weather, it wears away the

◀ A foliose or leaf-like lichen growing on a tree trunk.

▶ 'Pixie cups' lichen. The white funnels are spore-bearing structures called pycnidia, which produce spores that grow into fungal hyphae.

rock. The fungus part of the lichen can also eat away at the rock by producing acids. The minute particles of rock dislodged by the lichen help to form soil, on which other plants will eventually grow.

Lichens are useful

The reindeer of northern Europe and the caribou of North America depend on lichens during the long winter months when there is little other vegetation for them to feed on. The Eskimos of northern Canada ate the part-digested lichens they found in the stomachs of caribou and musk oxen. This may sound disgusting, but during the long cold northern winters it was probably the only way they had of getting any sort of vegetable food. In contrast, desert people in Iran mix lichens with meal to make into a kind of bread.

Many birds use lichens to make their nests. The European long-tailed tit and the parula warbler of North America make their nests almost entirely out of lichens.

Lichens have been used as dyes for many hundreds of years. People in Scotland and Ireland use lichens to dye cloth a whole range of shades from yellows and browns to reds and purples.

▲ In most parts of the world lichens are found in places where other plants find it difficult to grow. But in tropical regions, such as here, lichens grow anywhere.

By overdyeing one colour with another, for example a yellow with an indigo blue, they can make green. Some of the famous Harris tweed cloth of the Orkney islands is still made using lichen dyes.

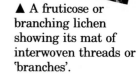

▲ A fruticose or branching lichen showing its mat of interwoven threads or 'branches'.

◄ This crustose lichen forms a hard flat crust on a rock. It has probably taken many, many years for the lichen to reach this size.

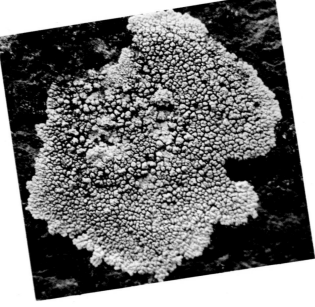

PLANT PARASITES

Many fungi live on other plants, especially on dying trees. They may speed up the death of their host and, by doing so, kill their source of food. But, by the time this happens, millions of their spores will have settled and grown into new fungi elsewhere. Apart from fungi, there are many plants that depend on other plants for their nourishment. The most spectacular is a plant called *Rafflesia*, which grows on vines in Malaysia – usually on their roots, but sometimes on their aerial stems. It produces the largest flower in the world, about 1 m (3 ft) across.

There are about 100 kinds of parasitic plants called dodders. This plant only has roots after it germinates, to give it support. After this it twines itself around other plants and sends out suckers called

haustoria into the tissues of the host plant. In North America, dodders damage crops such as alfalfa and lucerne, and in tropical areas they harm many trees. In Europe, a common dodder can be found climbing around plants such as gorse and heathers. The stem of this particular plant consists of fine crimson threads with small bunches of red and white flowers. The flowers of some dodders smell of rotten meat to attract the flies which pollinate them.

Broomrapes, another type of parasitic plant, are fleshy, up to 1 m (3 ft) high and of various colours – yellow, brown, reddish, mauve, even blue but never green. Like the dodders, they lack leaves and obtain all their nourishment from the roots of other plants. Broomrapes tend to be parasitic on plants of the pea family, especially broom. There are records that one North American broomrape provided food for an Indian tribe.

Half-parasites
There are also those plants that are partly parasitic – they can manufacture some of their own food, but depend on other plants for water and mineral salts. In most cases you would never tell by looking at them that they had a secret food supply, because it is through their roots that they attach themselves to other plants. One common exception is mistletoe, which grows from the branches of trees. A common kind is found on apple and poplar trees, but other mistletoes grow on larches, pines and firs.

The figwort family contains many half-parasitic plants, including the red and yellow rattles, eyebrights, and red and yellow bartsias, all of which look just like normal flowering plants.

◀ This strange-looking plant is called tall broomrape. It is parasitic on the roots of plants called knapweeds, which are relatives of the dandelion.

▶ Bracket fungi growing on a beech tree. What you see here are the fruiting bodies of the fungus – strands of fungal tissue called hyphae penetrate into the tissues of the tree, obtaining nourishment from them.

THE FUTURE

CONSERVATION OF WILD PLANTS

Plants are in danger through human activities. To feed more and more people, wild areas of forest and woodland are cleared, swamps and marshes are drained to make way for agricultural land. Forests are cut for timber. At the same time new buildings and roads are built – concrete is gradually filling in our breathing spaces, our wild places. The story is not only sad, it is dangerous because we depend so much on wild plants.

An estimated 25,000 different kinds of plants are in some way endangered. That is one in ten of all known flowering plants. It is sometimes difficult to realize just how drastic the situation is because most of the worst destruction is happening in places far away.

Tropical forest destruction
Probably the most endangered habitats are the tropical rainforests. Each year an area three times the size of Switzerland disappears. If this continues at the present rate all the rainforests will have gone by the end of the century. In the Amazon, a huge highway 5,600 km (3,500 miles) long is cutting a wide swathe through the forest. On either side of this

massive road, vast estates are cleared for cattle ranching. Similar projects are eating away the forests of Africa and south-east Asia.

We know how valuable these forests are as a source of plants for food, medicines and a great many other uses. Once plants become extinct there will never be any means of telling just what resources have been lost. At the same time as western influences reach these once remote areas, the native peoples become displaced and their traditional tribal societies destroyed. These peoples have lived close to nature for thousands of years and have a special knowledge of the plants that grow around them. Maybe one day we will need to call on this knowledge – but it could be too late!

Islands
Plants on islands are special because they have developed in isolation from the plants of the nearest mainland. Many of these are strange-looking, often beautiful. They are especially vulnerable to disturbance.

Hawaii is a good example of an island system whose original plants as well as animals have been and are being

► The trans-Amazonian highway is a massive motorway project undertaken by the Brazilian Government. It has already provided jobs for many people and much of the nearby forest has been settled. But it is doing enormous damage to the plants and animals of the forest and the local peoples who have lived there undisturbed for many centuries.

destroyed. Of the 2,200 kinds of plant native to the islands, 273 are already extinct and a further 800 are endangered. One reason for their disappearance, a problem common to all islands, is that over 3,000 plants from other places have been introduced, agricultural plants, garden flowers and weeds – plants that have crowded out the interesting original flora which had not been used to such competition. Areas of lush lowland forest have been cleared to provide crop-growing land. Industry, military bases and tourist developments also have killed off much of the natural vegetation.

Small dry islands, such as Socotra off the Horn of Africa, have suffered because of the introduction of goats. Socotra is the home of a wild pomegranate plant. Only a handful of these plants survive and they have no chance of reproducing properly because of the goats which quickly eat up any new seedlings that appear.

Saving plants

It is easy to describe how many plants are threatened, but it is a much more difficult task to help to save them. Many countries have set aside large areas of land as national parks and reserves to protect the wild plants and animals in them. The National Park system in the United States is a very good example. Unfortunately, not all the parks scattered throughout the world are maintained properly. In many countries where food and water are scarce and the standard of living is not as high as in more developed countries, protecting plants and animals seems a silly luxury. A worldwide approach to the problem is through education. People can be taught, from an early age, the value and beauty of plants, knowledge which they will then pass on to *their* children. Try to find out more yourselves by joining a local conservation society or wildlife group. Organizations such as the World Wildlife Fund help save thousands of acres of coutryside each year. *You* can help, because such organizations only have the success they do thanks to the enthusiasm of their members – and membership is open to anyone interested in their vital work.

▼ Rainforest vegetation growing along the coast of Maui, Hawaii. Much of the original forest has been destroyed.

GLOSSARY

Angiosperm Scientific name for a flowering plant; the seeds of these plants are protected by seed cases.

Annual A plant that completes its life cycle – growing, flowering and producing seeds in one year.

Anther The part of the stamen (the male part of a flower) which carries the pollen.

Biennial Plants with a two-year life cycle. They sprout one year, and flower, form seeds and die the following year.

Botanists Scientists who study plants.

Bract A leaf-like structure (usually small) found either at the base of the flower stalk or at the base of the flower head.

Bulb A special type of bud which, when planted in the ground, sends roots down from its base and shoots upwards from the middle of its tightly-packed body of special leaves. Daffodils and tulips grow from bulbs.

Carpel The female parts of a flowering plant: the stigma, style and ovary.

Cell The smallest unit of life. Plants are usually composed of thousands of cells, although there are microscopic single-celled plants.

Chlorophyll The substance in plants that gives them their green colouring.

Chloroplast Part of a plant cell that contains chlorophyll.

Corm A special underground stem that looks rather like a bulb but without the layers. Crocuses grow from corms.

Deciduous Plants, usually trees, that shed all their leaves each year, usually in the autumn or fall.

Dicotyledon Botanical name for a plant that produces two tiny leaves from the seed after germination.

Endosperm The part of a seed where food is stored to nourish the new plant when it starts to grow.

Enzyme Special substances in digestive juices that help break down food into a form that the plant can absorb and use.

Epiphyte A plant that grows on another but does not get any nourishment from the plant on which it is growing.

Evaporation The process which changes water from its liquid and visible form into invisible water vapour.

Evergreen A plant that keeps its leaves throughout the winter.

Evolution The gradual development of different forms of life.

Fertilization The joining of male and female sex cells to form the seed from which a new plant can develop.

Food chain A series of organisms which all depend on one another for food. A chain could start with tiny organisms such as algae, that are eaten by tiny fish, that are eaten by larger fish and so on, perhaps all the way to a large shark.

Fossil The remains of plants and animals that lived in past ages found in rocks or dug out of the ground.

Gamete The sex cell of a plant, such as a moss, which reproduces in two separate stages.

Gametophyte A plant, such as a moss, that produces gametes.

Germinate/germination When a seed puts out roots and shoots.

Graft Insert a bud or shoot from one plant into the stem of another, so that the two will grow together as one plant.

Gymnosperm Plants, such as conifers, whose seeds do not have the protection of any sort of seed pod.

Monocotyledon Botanical name for a

▼ When the seeds of the paeony are ripe, the protective seed case splits open and the seeds spill out. They fall to the ground and will be dispersed by birds and animals.

◄The cohosh, or snakeroot, from North America is an angiosperm with a long spike of small tight-packed flowers in which the stamens are most prominent.

plant that produces only one tiny leaf from the seed when it germinates.

Mycelium The mass of branching underground threads that connect the fruiting bodies of a cluster of fungi.

Osmosis The process by which plants absorb water from the soil through their roots.

Ovary The lowest part of the carpel which contains the plant's seed or seeds.

Ovule The immature fruit of a plant as it is contained in the ovary before fertilization.

Parasite Plant (or animal) that lives on another living plant (or animal) and gets all its food from that plant or animal.

Perennial A plant that lives for more than two years.

Photosynthesis The process by which plants make food.

Plumule The part of the fertilized seed that will develop into the first stem and leaf.

Pollinate/pollination The transfer of the male pollen cells to the female cells of a flower so that seeds can be formed.

Radicle The part of the fertilized seed that will develop into the first root.

Respiration Taking in oxygen and giving out carbon dioxide; a process which happens in all cells.

Saprophyte A plant that lives on dead or decaying plant or animal matter.

Sepals The outer casing of a flower bud.

Shrub A perennial with a tough, woody stem and branches close to the ground. It has no obvious trunk, like a tree, and is also smaller, but it is larger than a bush.

Species A group of plants or animals that look alike and behave in the same way, and are different from any others.

Sporangium (plural **sporangia**) The special case in which spores develop in plants such as ferns.

Spores Minute reproductive cells produced by some plants, including fungi.

Sporophyte The part of a moss plant that produces spores in the second part of the plant's two-generation life-cycle.

Stamen The male, pollen-bearing part of a flower.

Stigma The top part of the style.

Stoma (plural **stomata**) Minute pores or openings in the surface of a leaf.

Style The stalk connecting the stigma and the ovary.

Symbiosis An association between two different living organisms from which both benefit. Lichens, which consist of an alga and a fungus, are a good example.

Tundra The vast Arctic regions in the northern hemisphere where there are no trees and only very small low-growing plants. Only the surface of the ground ever thaws.

Vegetation Plants and plant life.

▼ The Petrified Forest National Park in Arizona, USA, has the largest collection of remains of petrified (fossilized) wood in the world. These fossil trees date back to the Triassic period which began 225 million years ago.

Acknowledgments

A–Z Botanical Collection, Heather Angel, Ardea, Australian News & Information Service, Bautier, Ron Boardman, A Borgioli & G Cappeli, Paul Brierley, NA Callow, Bruce Coleman, Gene Cox, Daily Telegraph Colour Library, Douglas Dickins, Foto Dulevant, Durand, Explorer, Gilardi, Archivio IGDA, Kayebon Press Ltd Cheshire, Roger Kohn, Frank Lane, Marka, NHPA M Pedone, Picturepoint, A Pitcairn/Grant Heilman, Richard Revels, SEF, J Six & M Buzzini, Spectrum Colour Library, John Watney, Trevor Wood.